Shweta Suresh Rana

Dr. George Tumanishvili

Ageism: The New Type of Discrimination

Meaning, Causes and Ways to Fight

Caucasus University
Tbilisi, 2021

AGEISM: THE NEW TYPE OF DISCRIMINATION
MEANING, CAUSES AND WAYS TO FIGHT

Shweta Suresh Rana
Dr. George G. Tumanishvili

ISBN: 978-9941-9702-9-0

Published by Caucasus University Publishing House

Correspondence:
Shweta Suresh Rana - shwetascsrana@gmail.com
Dr. George G. Tumanishvili - georgetumanishvili@gmail.com

Shweta Suresh Rana [1]

Dr. D.Y. Patil College of Law, Mumbai University

Dr. George Tumanishvili [2]

Caucasus University, Caucasus School of Law

Abstract

This book discusses issues and topics of which the importance is growing day by day. The expression of a person's talents and abilities should not be restricted by age. Ageism is a complex problem related to the fields of psychology, sociology and law, as well as to the many stigmas ingrained in many societies. The presented book discusses Ageism from different angles, including, and focusing on the legal side. The attitudes of various segments of society towards the issue are studied, and the conclusions are made. The study is significant and relevant to a broad range of readers and aims to raise awareness and rethink existing attitudes and social standards towards Ageism.

---

[1] For correspondence: shwetascsrana@gmail.com
[2] For correspondence: georgetumanishvili@gmail.com

Contents

Introduction and definition - Answering "What?"

"Age is just a number." Although that is what is told to us, in reality, society doesn't follow this convention. Ever wondered why people associate their life-plans and accomplishments to age as if life is a game that has various levels that need to be cleared within a time limit. If deadlines are crossed, you will be demoted to the previous level or lose one of the three lives you get at the start of the game. The idea behind this perspective is fairly conventional. What has been going on, shall be continued. Human beings resist change. It is intriguing to know that various systems of belief are deep-rooted with the concept of crediting age more than it needs to be. There is a widely accepted international classification of the population based on age. One of the sets of classifications deals essentially with six broad population groups - roughly equivalent to infancy, youth, young adulthood, middle adulthood, and older adulthood to average retirement age, and retirement (under 1, 1-14, 15-

24, 25-44, 45-64 and 65 years). Those age groups allow aggregation from the two previous sets of classifications.[3]

There are mainly two approaches that are taken while defining 'ageism'. One is as defined by Butler in "The Encyclopedia of Aging" published in the year 1987, "Ageism is defined as the process of systematic stereotyping of, and discrimination against, people because they are old just as sexism and racism accomplish this for gender and skin color".[4] And the other approach is as defined by Itzin, "Ageism is usually regarded as being something that affects the lives of older people. Like ageing, however, it affects every individual from birth onwards- at every stage putting limits and constraints on experience, expectations, relationships, and opportunities. Its divisions are as arbitrary as those of

---

[3] *Provisional Guidelines on Standard International Age Classifications.* (n.d.). Retrieved February 8, 2021, from https://unstats.un.org/unsd/publication/SeriesM/SeriesM _74e.pdf

[4] Butler, R. N. (2009). Combating ageism. In *International Psychogeriatrics* (Vol. 21, Issue 2, p. 211). Cambridge University Press. https://doi.org/10.1017/S104161020800731X

race, gender, class, and religion. Thus, the chronology of ageing becomes the hierarchy of ageism.[5] Wherein the former approach advocates the existence of prejudice against people who are considered as "old" by society. They stand against the discrimination that the "old" aged people face due to the attitudes of others and the bias expressed towards them. Whereas the latter supports the existence of the bias that is faced by all ages due to the discriminatory attitudes of people that have been formed as a result of cultures that have developed due to societal standards and expectations which are associated with every age group. These standards are considered to be the ideal standards that have to be met by one, to be accepted as fit or normal.

Although it is fair to say that both approaches do not aim to criticize the other and thus, are not exclusive of each other. The second approach is inclusive of the first. Thus, it is fair to assume that the second approach is more viable

---

[5] Maddox, G. (2001). The Encyclopedia of Aging. In *The Encyclopedia of Aging*. Springer Berlin Heidelberg. https://doi.org/10.1007/978-3-662-38338-4

keeping the present times in perspective. It may be possible that the period in which the first approach gained popularity was due to the majority of the population belonging to the "old" age group. The difficulties faced were highlighted with the "old-ageism" which became a more accepted concept.

Times have changed and so have the problems. The world has become cruel to not just one age, but all. With various kinds of expectations being associated with a certain age group, it becomes pressurizing for a human being to meet those needs of the society. Not only that such discrimination is demotivating an individual, but it also restrains the abilities of an individual to do better and perform to do the best of her potential.

Jurisprudence

"Salus populi suprema lex"[6]

According to Cicero "the health of the people is the supreme law." [7] The welfare of the people is and shall be the supreme law. Doing what's best for the people and shall continue to be the intention of creating laws in the state. It is the greater good, that will be chosen above everything. This legal maxim is the inspiration and ideology of this paper. The need to acknowledge the plight of the victims of this discrimination will help to spread awareness in the society. This consciousness will lead to change, thus, making the lives of the people better and resulting in their welfare and peace of their mental health.

---

[6] "The health (welfare, good, salvation, felicity) of the people should be the supreme law".
[7] Witt, J. (n.d.). *The Law of Salus Populi | The Yale Review*. Retrieved February 8, 2021, from https://yalereview.yale.edu/law-salus-populi

Classification of ageism -Answering "How?"

Moving forward, it is important to understand the types of ageism to fully cover this topic. Discrimination is of different types. Ageism is that kind of discrimination that is based on age. Further, ageism is classified into more types. The broadest categories are positive (for the aged) and negative ageism (against the elders). Age bias in the workplace, societal prejudice towards people of a certain age, the potential judgment of people based on their age, are few of such broad categories.

Ageism includes both prejudice (beliefs and attitudes) and discrimination (actions). Thus, there are 4 types of ageism-:[8]

1. Negative prejudice

    a. Negative stereotypes (beliefs)

        i. The belief that most aged are sick

        ii. Impotent

        iii. Ugly

---

[8] Palmore, E. B. (1999). *Ageism: Negative and Positive, 2nd Edition - Erdman Palmore, PhD - Google Books.*

       iv.   Senile

       v.   Mentally ill

       vi.   Useless

       vii.   Isolated

       viii.   Poor

       ix.   depressed

    b. Negative attitudes (feelings)

2. Negative discrimination

3. Positive prejudice

    a. Kind

    b. Wise

    c. Dependable

    d. Affluent

    e. Politically powerful

    f. Free

    g. Happy

4. Positive discrimination

    a. Economical

    b. Family

    c. Housing

    d. Health care

Further, the study referred goes on to explain personal ageism by individuals and institutional ageism, by institutions and social structures.

Many surveys and reports have been drafted to highlight the discrimination faced by people based on their age, in their everyday lives. One such report is [9]

Table 1.[10]

Percentages Reporting Types of Ageism (N = 84)

% Reporting

Item	0	1	2+	Event
1	42	17	42	Told a joke that pokes fun

[9] Palmore, E. B. (1999). *Ageism: Negative and Positive, 2nd Edition - Erdman Palmore, PhD - Google Books*.
[10] Palmore, E. (2001). The Ageism Survey: First findings. In *Gerontologist* (Vol. 41, Issue 5, pp. 572–575). Gerontological Society of America. https://doi.org/10.1093/geront/41.5.572

2	70	12	18	Sent a birthday card that pokes fun
3	69	15	15	Ignored or not taken seriously
4	82	10	8	Called an insulting name
5	61	20	19	Patronized or "talked down to"
6	99	0	1	Refused rental housing
7	92	5	4	Difficulty getting a loan
8	92	7	1	Denied a position of leadership

9	82	8	10	Rejected as unattractive
10	70	10	20	Treated with less dignity and respect
11	89	6	5	Waiter or waitress ignored
12	57	24	19	Doctor or nurse assumed ailments caused by age
13	92	4	5	Denied medical treatment
14	95	5	0	Denied employment
15	90	8	1	Denied promotion

16	67	13	20	Assumed I could not hear well
17	69	14	17	Assumed I could not understand
18	57	17	26	Told me, "You're too old for that."
19	95	4	1	House vandalized
20	95	2	2	Victimized by a criminal
Mean	78	10	11	

Percentages may not add up to 100 because of rounding.

Previous measures of ageism included: the Attitudes Towards Old People Scale (Kogan 1961); the Fraboni Scale of Ageism (Fraboni et al. 1990) measuring the affective component of ageism; the Palmore Ageism

Survey (Palmore 2001); a prescriptive ageism scale (North and Fiske 2013) focusing on prescriptive beliefs concerning potential intergenerational conflicts. Most of these tools measure the cognitive and affective dimensions of ageism and are not designed to study workplace discrimination. Yet, this is the aim of the Nordic Age Discrimination Scale (Furunes and Mykletun 2010), which incorporates six items that are supposed to measure the perception of age discrimination among employees. However, it does not assess the experiences of age discrimination among older workers, which might still be disparate from the general view of employees about age discrimination in their workplace.[11]

---

[11] Stypinska, J., & Turek, K. (2017). Hard and soft age discrimination: the dual nature of workplace discrimination. *European Journal of Ageing, 14*(1), 49–61. https://doi.org/10.1007/s10433-016-0407-y

Survey conducted to determine the understanding and relation of the phenomenon of Ageism

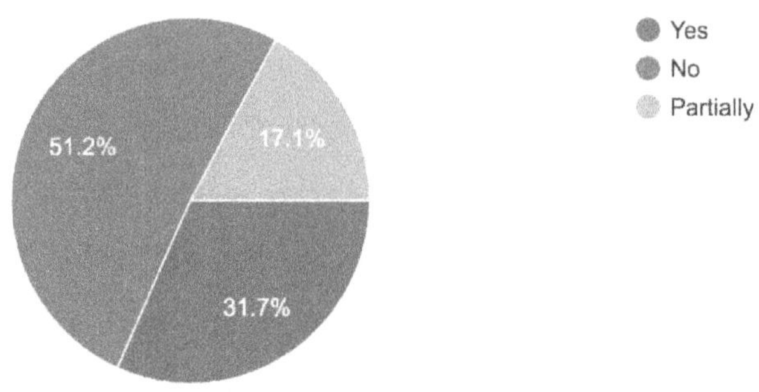

For a better understanding of the concerns that are coming from the different parts of the society and are redistributed across the globe and nationalities, also, among the different cultural and age groups we ran a survey. We asked our respondents if they considered age to be important when it comes to a job or relationships, to which 51.2 % answered in the negative, 31.7% in the affirmative, and 17.1% were not sure. Question: Do you consider age to be important for getting a new job or in regard to the relationship between people?

It is interesting that when we asked if they were aware of what "ageism" is, it was surprising to note the results.

Despite not being the most popular concept, the respondents were briefly aware of what age discrimination is. Question: Do you know what ageism or age

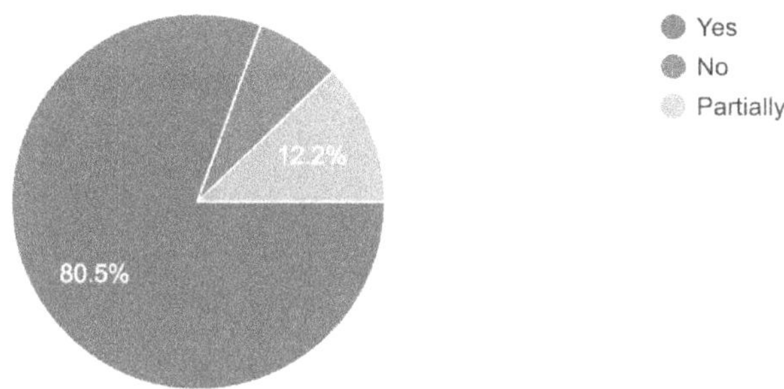

discrimination is?

Then we put forward certain statements relating to age and asked our respondents if they believed in them or not and requested them to share their personal experience by explaining their belief and what they understood by the statement. Some interesting answers have been mentioned-:

"There is an age for everything".

"In a society, we are expected to respond to it in a particular way so that we get accepted by society. Eg. If a person would want to learn some specific thing which he could have learned at an earlier age, it would be a bit

difficult for him/her to associate himself with the people who are dominating at that place. The subjugating behavior of the crowd and the society will not definitely but to an extent hamper the performance of the person." Furthermore, there were groups of answers such as *"Age teaches you a lot of things that can only be learned that way".* One of the respondents even mentioned what they believed comes with age," *Performance, making mistakes, being more tolerant, getting patient, doing not so many brave things, less energy and more peace."*

Among the respondents, there were many who disagreed, *"There is a most popular answer for this question, Warren Buffet became a billionaire at age of 50-60s where on other hand there are many startups whose founder became a successful entrepreneur at a very young age", "simple evidence is that there are books or other educational materials about the same topic but are different for primary school pupils, for secondary school pupils and so on. As for adult life, age plays a less important role and I can say, for adults, age means nothing"*

One even responded, "I do not identify with age. Experience determines maturity and not age. Even a 40-year-old person may be less mature than a 20-year-old person depending on experience and exposure. I am a 24-year-old, but I lack the experience of an average 24-year-old. This is the case with me in everything I am involved in." and the other answered as *"When it comes to learning or becoming independent in terms of your finances or personal decisions age is not a barrier. Obviously with age comes experience which is a strong boost to any field but that doesn't mean you can't do it. You might fail because of lack of age but failure itself is the biggest teacher",* *"Not a personal experience but in general, there are age limits in our education system. So, if a person crosses that age, he/she is most likely to be unable to redo it. But again, on the other hand, there are people who realize their passions and ambitions at quite later stages of their lives and still start from scratch and achieve zeniths"* and many such.

1.   "Old people are rigid in their attitude", "Old people are wise", etc.

Few agreed and answered *"The more one ages with a concept, one tends to believe some things longer, and eventually, the belief turns into fact. The LGBTQIA community is not accepted by all. Religious belief is also one such thing. Grandparents kneel down during prayer. Considering their physical condition, it is not advisable. Kneeling down on hard surfaces is not a healthy practice when it comes to the knee as it can compress and damage bursitis. They still do it because they believe."* and one responded, *"With age, they have a lot of experience of life and these experiences make them set a certain rule book about what is wrong and what is right and because they are intransigent about it because they made those rules based on THEIR experience."* Some disagreed *"Old people have spent a greater amount of time with a certain belief or in a certain way so it might be difficult (not for all) to adjust to changes but they do overcome that in a while, each in their own pace."*

Related to the wisdom - *"Because of the fact that they have spent a lot more time than us working or accomplishing goals in a distraction-free environment back then, they tend to be focused and can make better-informed decisions as compared to today's generation.",* and some had a critical approach *"I could say that some old people are wise, the ones that work on educating themselves on a daily basis, on the ones that took some time to think about different things on a deeper level. But the ones who haven't done anything in their lives, but being lazy and having all the same people around them, shouldn't be considered wise. Because usually, they can't even explain why they think the way they think"*

2. *"Young people are lazy", Young people are impulsive", etc.*

Few agreed, *"I believe with so many distractions around it is possible to easily get derailed and lose focus on what a person is trying to achieve.", "They lack guidance and motivation to take the right steps."*

Many defended and disagreed, key responses being "*I think that line is just a stereotype set by the older generation. There are so many young people excelling in their fields, studying and working simultaneously. They are never lazy if they're working towards something that they're passionate about.*" and "*Because age doesn't define how hardworking a person is. Young person has a life to build and we would not see so many young, successful entrepreneurs who chose to find new way than to stick to older generation's road if this statement was true*"

When asked about impulsiveness "*Cause even though some young people can be more experienced professionally, or have more knowledge than the older ones, the energy they have and the life experience they have is usually less than the one that older people do. So I would say that other youngsters as myself, need more life experience and self-awareness in order not to be impulsive when it's not needed.*" and defended the young "*All that zeal and excitement of doing new things and trying new experiences makes them take in the moment and keep them* *from seeing through it.''*And few disagreed, *"Impulsiveness is a character trait. Most scientists and researchers I have met are very impulsive (that too about the same field they have been working in for decades)."*

We asked our respondents more questions, that allows them to reflect and identify their own ageist behavior.

Have you ever reflected your opinions about age by your behavior or words towards anyone?

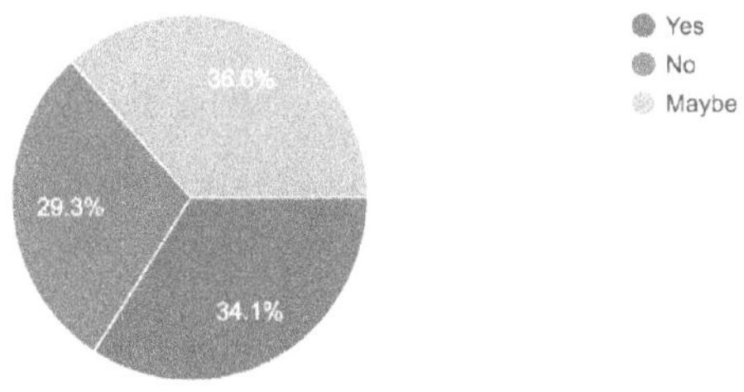

Have you ever passed any such comment/gesture at anyone?

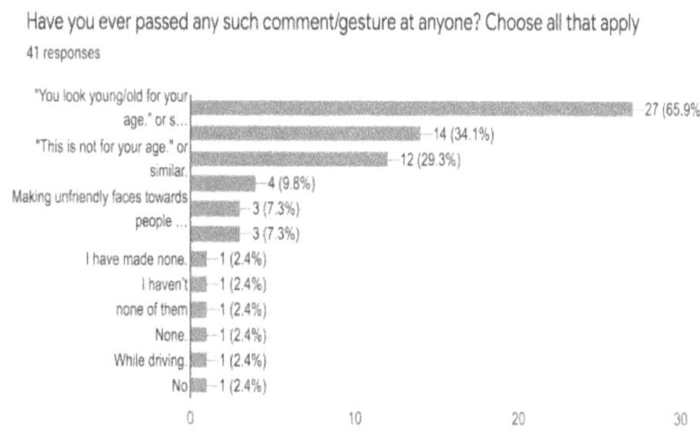

We asked them to share their experience of ageism, as an unintentional bully or victim. The responses were interesting to note. Could you please share the context wherein you passed such unkind gestures or comments intentionally/unintentionally at an old/young person? There were notable confessions, *"My team leader aged 45+ is trying to do tasks that he's not supposed to do as they can be delegated. However, when I reflect on this, I feel by doing this he either tries to achieve high deliverable standards or its his nature to make sure tasks are done more effectively & efficiently, as others might end up spending more than required time & efforts." "I prefer to be positive and don't have prejudices, but sometimes I make this comment without realizing that it may be*

offensive to a person". "Looking at the younger generation a lot of times it has happened mostly because of their behavior or just tend to compare my childhood with today's toddlers.", "When people complain about their age and their appearance, I'm usually the one that tells them "Why u even worry, u look 10 years younger!". I've never said that someone looks older for their age, because it might make them feel bad."

Question: Do you think the person at whom you expressed your views about their age, might be hurt by it?

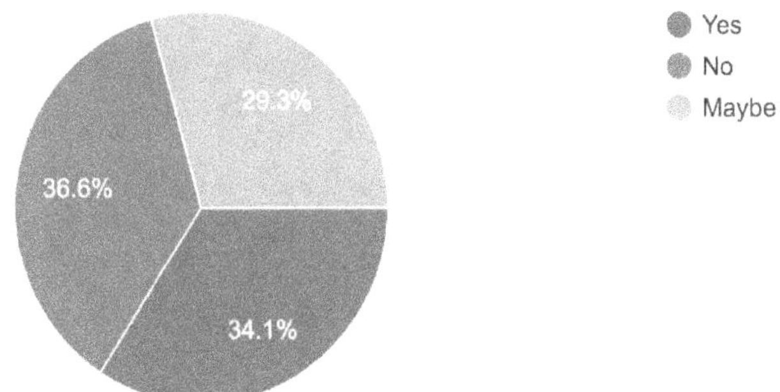

We asked respondents if they can express their views, on how they would feel, if they are in the shoes of a person at whom such discriminatory and ageist views are expressed?

"Frustrated," "I'll feel bad," "Uncomfortable," "It would have been a very unpleasant feeling"., "Lower self-confidence," "I will be angry," "Might feel demotivated in terms of capacity and capability.," "Its feeling of not able to make the other person understand you capabilities.", „A sense of underestimation.,", "I process too much about what people think about me. My age might give me anxiety" were common answers.

One of the respondents answered with his personal experience, *"I can tell you how I always feel when I'm a victim of ageism on a daily basis. So when my classmates and university mates were studying, I was working and studying, learning something else and studying. So today when they are doing their internships to start their career, I'm already working, having a competitive salary and position. Some would say that's amazing and I would agree, but the thing is then when people see me, they are like: "Are u still in school?", "Which university are you going to?", "What do you want to become?", "You are still young, you will find a job", "If you find a job for 500 USD*

it will be great for your age (I make minimum 4k/month)"
etc."

When we asked them, "why do you think your perspective about people of a certain age is like the way it is?" One responded, *"Partially maybe due to the societal conditioning and partially due to incidences I have witnessed that reinforces the assumptions (not sure)"*, *"Because I have absorbed it from the society around me it comes naturally. Like oh this your age you should be doing this certain job or work according to your age. Which I feel is wrong, it should be left on the person."* All these answers directed that society has a big role to play in this issue.

Question: Are you willing to change your ageist behavior? Then finally we asked our respondents, what they are the solutions to ageism and what should be done, and this is how they responded. *"Become more acceptive of everyone and understand that life isn't same for everyone"* *"Awareness about this issue at every place and discussing it with everyone so that people get to know that such a*

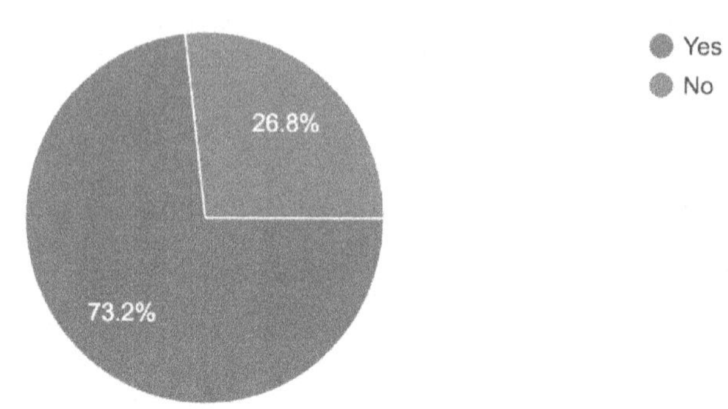

thing exists.", For starters- I would try to be mindful before passing any comment(s) when in a diverse group of people.", Having people of different age around me and seeing that they also don't seclude themselves and have motivation to be part of "our" young society".

Question: Have you ever experienced ageism?

We requested them to share their experiences. And this is how they answered, *"In my experience it involves mostly sphere of private life (time to get married, have kids and in general settle down) and also in profession, aka being intern when you are 24-25 is something surprising, studying new profession after the same age is also looked upon", "It's like people crack jokes about not being so fit*

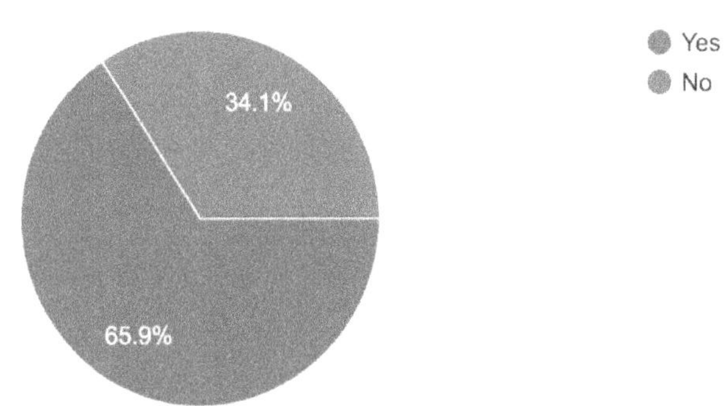

or active according to age and also misjudge sometimes."

and many such.

Question: How many times have you experienced ageism or seen it?

When asked about statements used at them reflecting ageist behavior, following were the responses

"You're too old to do this;

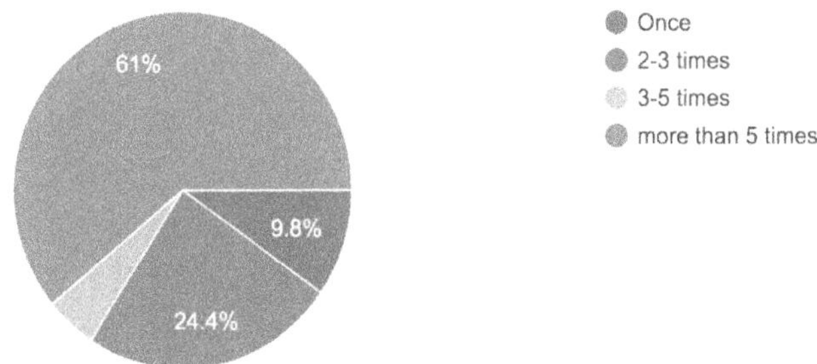

You're young, you should be able to do this;

You're so young, you can't have an opinion;

You're too old, you have no clue about our generation;

"You are too old for this. You will he the granny among your classmates";

"Will you get married when you are on the way to your grave?";

"You have missed all the age milestones for achievement. You have ruined your life";

"How can you marry a lady who is older than you by 3 years!";

Those are some of the statements I remember people telling me and people I know."

Question: *Has this or these discriminatory occurrences caused any kind?*

Question: *Do you feel triggered by anything similar to that day when you were discriminated against (could be a word, place or person?*

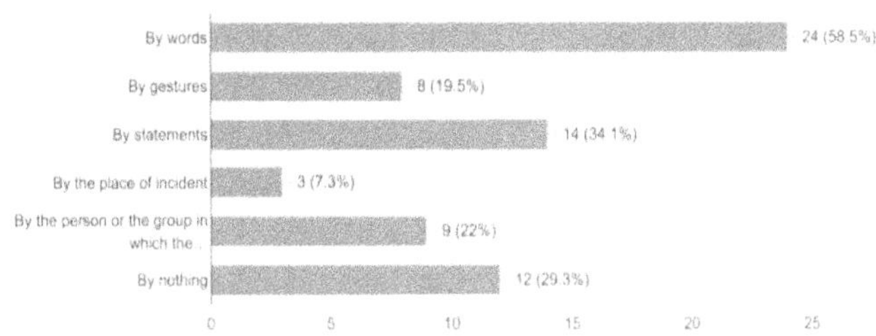

Does this fear affect your performance at your workplace or in any environment?

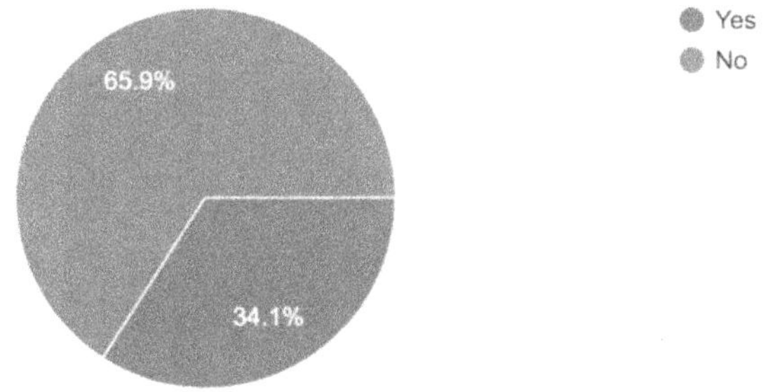

Do you think there should be a better system of criteria set to determine the worth of a candidate for a title, instead of focusing on age?

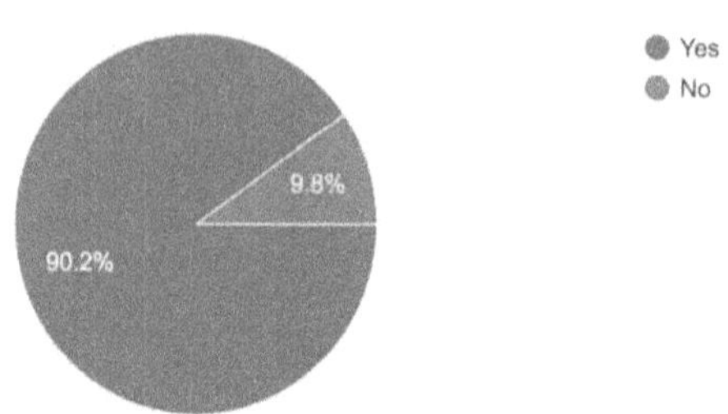

Do you think victims of such discrimination, miss out on opportunities that they deserve due to ageism?

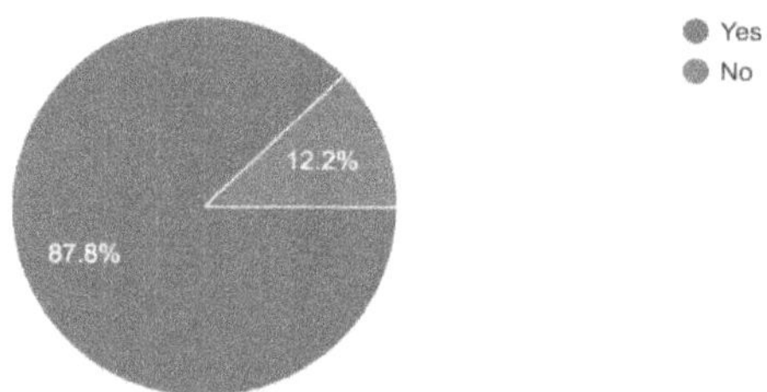

Do you think we need laws to prevent this age discrimination?

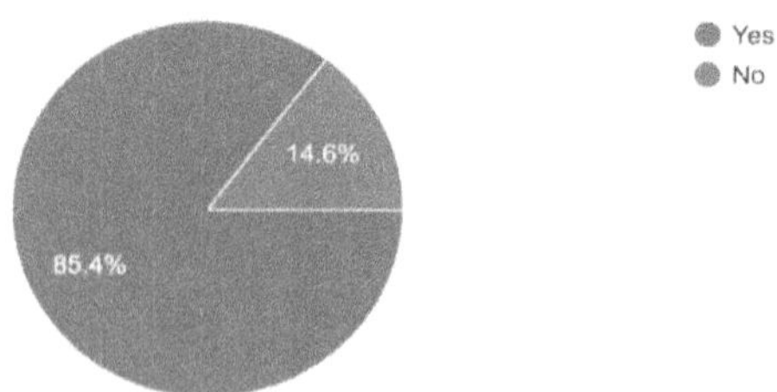

On the question "What kind of laws do you think can prevent ageism? ", most of the answers were around

"Personal laws , workplace laws, removing age from admission process etc.", "Proper legislation to protect the interest of all kinds of people at different strata of the society.", "There can be some laws to prevent ageism at workplace like zero tolerance against ageism","Anti-discrimination laws and changing the labor code", "No retirement age limit", "The laws that fine employers and employees in case of age discrimination at any workplace.", "In India, marriage laws have different ages for men and women to get married. The entrance exams and educational opportunities are also dependent on age sometimes. Those rules should be taken down. Knowledge should be available to all irrespective of age.", "Person should be hired or fired based on their performance rather than just age factor . There should be laws which will prevent ageism and give more opportunities to all kinds of people based on their performance rather than age."

Aspects of conventional laws due to ageism

Laws are framed in a society, according to the needs of the members of that society. Certain laws turn obsolete and thus, are abrogated. Some laws need amendments and with necessary changes, they are made more adaptable to the society. At times, as observed with the legal history, reforms were necessary due to the discriminatory nature of certain laws towards a particular section by including or excluding them. This discrimination is at times unintended due to lack of awareness of the bias and the issues of that section of people.

However, in the vast majority of circumstances throughout our society, adults are treated most favorably. Adult centrism is a dominant feature throughout communities, governments, homes and families, faith-based communities, and even schools. Adult centrism is based on adultism, which is being biased towards adults. This bias is the central force in causing the three resultant phenomena of pedophobia, which is the fear of children; ephebiphobia, which is fear of youth; and gerontophobia, which is fear of older people. While all of these are reliant on each other for their emphasis and power, each is rooted in the primary bias towards adults. The relationships between age discriminations consistently favoring adults leads to these discriminations in a variety of ways. Namely, adultism is used internally by individuals to justify their fears of alternating age groups of which they don't belong or don't favor.[12]

Before the early 1970s, the area of legal inquiry that is today referred to as "elder law" or "law and aging" was virtually unknown in the field of law (Levine 1982; Bogutz 2008). Equally, the study of the relationships and interconnections between law, older persons, and/or the aging process was latent in the debates of social gerontologists (Doron 2009). This state of affairs changed dramatically with the emergence, almost 50 years ago, in

---

[12] *Understanding the Causes of Age Discrimination – Freechild Institute.* (n.d.). Retrieved February 8, 2021, from https://freechild.org/2016/01/07/age-discrimination/

the United States, of "law and aging" as an autonomous field of legal scholarship and practice.

The emergence of law and aging as a field of legal studies and practice in the United States in the early 1970s can be ascribed to three factors: first, the demographic aging of the American population and the social changes that this wrought on all fields of life, demanding a social response; second, the awareness on the part of the private bar and private lawyers that their clients were growingly older. This has pushed lawyers from different branches of law to "specialize" in the field of elder law. Third, and finally, the academia and the research community at large realized the opportunity and need to explore this new field of law. As an outcome of the combination of these three factors, the field of "elder law" has become recognized as a unique field and expertise in law, in the United States in particular, with its specific law journals, professional bodies, as well as new programs and classes, have been established within law schools.

A starting point for discussing ageism from a positive, international human rights law perspective is arguably the Universal Declaration of Human Rights (UDHR), adopted by the United Nations (UN) General Assembly in 1948. The Universal Declaration of Human Rights recognizes that all humans are born free and equal in dignity and rights (art. 1). "Everyone", continues article 2, is entitled to all the rights and freedoms set forth in it, "without distinction of any kind, such as race, color, sex, language, religion, political or another opinion, national or social origin, property, birth or another status." While arguably, being "old" can certainly be covered under "other status" – it is interesting to note that "age" does not specifically appear in this article. Moreover, ageism can act as a barrier to the enjoyment of the inherent entitlement of all human beings to human rights, such as the right to an adequate standard of living, to health, to access justice, to live free from violence and abuse (OHCHR 2012). The stereotyping and discriminating against individuals or groups on the basis of their age (Butler 1975) may be "under the skin" of social norms and prejudices but lead to very concrete and overt age discrimination (Chung 2010, p.4; Herring 2009, p.12). Employers, for instance, who struggle with their own sense of aging, may more easily make discriminatory choices in hiring older persons. In 1996, General Comment (n. 6) of the Committee supervising, the Covenant on Economic Social and Cultural rights (IESCR) had clarified that the list of forbidden grounds of discrimination contained in the core human rights treaties must be interpreted as including age (CESCR 1996); 13 years later, in 2009, the same committee recognized age as a "prohibited ground of discrimination in several contexts", e.g., against unemployed older persons in finding work, in access to training and retraining, and on discrimination in access to universal old age pension due to place of residence" (our italics, CESCR 2009).[13]

---

[13] Doron, I., Numhauser-Henning, A., Spanier, B., Georgantzi, N., & Mantovani, E. (2018). Ageism and Anti-Ageism in the Legal System: A Review of Key Themes. In *International Perspectives on Aging* (Vol. 19, pp. 303–319). Springer, Cham. https://doi.org/10.1007/978-3-319-73820-8_19

Retirement is a prominent example where this bias is felt in various industries that stops and restrain people of a certain age to work and earn a living for themselves and their family. At times, the conventional system is followed that people of that age, need to retire due to their age and the medical requirements that come with it. It is assumed that work may cause mental strain on the aged people which is pressurizing for their age. This system is well intended but may not rest with the intentions every time because not everyone's situation is the same. This condition worsens when due to some reasons the person reaching the "retirement age" has no alternative sources of income.

Other areas of conventional laws where ageism is prominent are political careers, where there are laws that only allow people above 35 years of age are allowed to contest for elections, considering people below it unfit for the job due to their age. Such as according to <u>Article II of the U.S. Constitution</u>, the president must be a natural-born citizen of the United States, be at least 35 years old, and have been a resident of the United States for 14 years.[14] According to Article 58 of the Constitution, no person shall be eligible for election as President unless he is a citizen of India, has completed the age of thirty-five years, and is qualified for election as a member of the House of the People. [15]

We also find laws in which age is given importance more than it needs to be, considering it to be a major and sometimes sole factor of qualification or criteria. Take for instance marriage. The legal age of marriage in most countries is 18 years of age. Considering it to be the age where the step of marriage can be taken as an adult and that such responsibility can be easily handled. Sometimes such a decision is forced on the 18-year-olds which leads to mental and emotional pressure. [16]

---

[14] President's, Vice Presidents, and First Ladies of the United States | USAGov
[15] Parliament - Parliament - Election Commission of India
[16] Child Marriage and the Law - Girls Not Brides
https://www.girlsnotbrides.org/child-marriage-law/

Root cause of ageism -Answering "Why?"

In primitive societies, old age was frequently valued. (Simmons, 1945). Older persons often provided knowledge, experience, and institutional memory that was of adaptive – even survival – value to their societies. Although nomadic groups in various parts of the world abandoned the old and disabled when safety and security were at stake, overall older people were venerated. However, as the number and percentage of older persons, especially the frail and demented, increased, the perception grew that they were burdens to their families and society. This perception became widespread as societies shifted from agrarian economies, where older men had traditionally owned the land, to industrialized economies, where work was no longer centered in the home and older persons lost their authority.

However, it must be noted that the status of older persons and our attitudes toward them are not only rooted in historic and economic circumstances. They also derive from deeply held human concerns and fears about the vulnerability inherent in the later years of life. Such feelings can translate into contempt and neglect.[17]

Ageism is the stereotyping, prejudice, and discrimination against people on the basis of their age. Ageism is widespread and an insidious practice that has harmful effects on the health of older adults. For older people, ageism is an everyday challenge. Overlooked for employment, restricted from social services, and stereotyped in the media, ageism marginalizes and excludes older people in their communities. Ageism is everywhere, yet it is the most socially "normalized" of any prejudice and is not widely countered – like racism or sexism. These attitudes lead to the marginalization of

---

[17] Combating ageismPDF, Robert N. Butler, International Psychogeriatrics, 21, 2, 4 2009, available at https://www.cambridge.org/core/journals/international-psychogeriatrics/article/combating-ageism/6E57AFD8E0C465A9108E186B9254F8D3/core-reader.

older people within our communities and have negative impacts on their health and well-being.[18]

What is the reason behind this discrimination?

Terror management theory claims that humans possess cognitive abilities that allow them to be self-conscious, and that this self-consciousness is reflected in humans' awareness of their vulnerability and mortality, which creates the potential for a paralyzing terror. According to terror management theory, in order to manage the anxiety brought about by the awareness of mortality, humans unconsciously sustain faith in cultural worldviews, which enable them to portray human life as meaningful, important, and enduring. The adoption of social and cultural rules allows humans to believe that they are valuable and deserving within their culture. Perceived social approval leads humans to feel self-esteem, which is reflected in the belief that they are significant human beings in a meaningful world. These perceptions allow

---

[18] WHO | Ageism
http://www.who.int/ageing/ageism/en/

humans to buffer anxiety and to maintain relative equanimity despite their awareness of their vulnerability and mortality (Greenberg et al. 1997; Greenberg et al. 1986). Unlike proximal and conscious defenses, such as active suppression and cognitive distortion of death-related thoughts, self-esteem and worldview are not based on a logical or rational approach to death but provide symbolic and ongoing defenses which allow humans to construe themselves as valuable participants in a meaningful universe (Greenberg et al. 1994, 1997; Pyszczynski et al. 1999).

These findings stress the uniqueness of the relationship between social versus age groups and discrimination in different age groups. Whereas among social groups discrimination towards out-groups emerges from holding a different worldview, which can be perceived as a threat to the worldview of in-group members (Greenberg et al. 2002; Solomon et al. 2004), among age groups, the threat emerges from the possible similarity between members of the groups. This distinction emphasizes the unique nature of ageism, which is different from other forms of prejudice and discrimination and points to the necessity for generating unique hypotheses concerning its roots (Martens et al. 2004).

A less direct association of older adults and death is embedded in the deterioration of the physical body that is reflected in older adults' physical appearance (e.g., wrinkles), as well as in the physical and cognitive decline that is often seen in older age, and in the diminishing control over bodily functions that older adults often experience. These characteristics of old age remind us that, like all animals, we are flesh and blood creatures who are vulnerable to death (Martens et al. 2005). According to Isaksen (2002), the fear of encountering the deteriorating bodies of older adults might be particularly high in Western society. According to this belief, as regards bodies, all humans are alike. In contrast, soul and mind are perceived as unique features that define us on a social and cultural level and make us different and separate from one another. Thus, physical decline and diminishment of physical control among older adults create an emphasis on the physical self over the spiritual self and can symbolize the inability to impose mind over matter (Isaksen 2002).

Negative impact or aftermath of this discrimination

When understanding this concept of ageism, it is important to include a section that caters to the consequences of such discrimination, what impact it leaves on the victims and why does it, therefore, makes this discrimination serious enough to be removed from the society. It is a common perspective that the old are wiser than the young. Almost everyone we have met must have felt being targeted by ageism. If it is a young child of 10-15 years of age, he/she must have received comments from people that they are too young to do certain things, example being serious about what they want to be, or cook something, or take care of their fashion sense, or maybe simply being passionate enough about something to think of it as career, like a sports player.If it is a 15-25-year-old person, we often see them being called lazy, casual about life, non-serious, ill-focused, distracted, and naive. They are always termed to procrastinate things. It's not necessary that they are all these things. In fact, the contrary is a possibility. With so much information in hand, and so many knowledge-sources available, the kids today are nothing but more aware, informed, and alert about things around them. They have a sense of life, so early in their age, which is drastically different and more than the 20-year-olds of the 19th century. It is quite unfair to dismiss their life experiences and the knowledge they have gained over the years, just because they are not old. It is assumed that a 30-40-year-old needs to be well-settled. Have a house of themselves, a car to commute, be married, and have kids of which he/she takes care of, provides for, and nurtures. Be fully financially stable and strong, should be "ideal" and take care of his/her parents. It is assumed that they will have their life together if not all, at most times.

When it comes to 60 and above years old. It's an assumption that they might want to retire, stay at home at all times, and have answers and solutions to all the questions of life. But it's not necessary. There is a possibility that they might want to work more. Or even if they retire from work, they don't retire from life. They can be crazy and have fun and do adventurous things. Why does society restrict them to have a life then? They don't always have to be all-knowing, wise, calm, and composed, or grumpy, and arrogant. Why does it necessarily have to be that way?

Life does not treat everyone the same. Everyone is prone to different and wide-ranging incidents in their life. At present, there will be 20-year-olds, who have built a successful business, and are financially independent and smart. Or 20-year-olds, who are working 9-5, to meet the financial needs of their home, who are hard-working, focused, and responsible for their duties. There will be 35-year-olds, who don't have kids or maybe do, but are not married because they don't want to be. There will be 40-year-olds, somewhere, homeless and jobless at home, serving in nursing or doing social work, and living with their parents. Why does it always have to be a certain way?

Finally, ageism might evoke perceptions concerning the difficulty of preserving positive self-esteem in old age (Martens et al. 2005). According to terror management theory, self-esteem is a vital resource in human life, because it buffers the potential for death-related anxiety (Greenberg et al. 1986). Social perceptions and stereotypes often associate old age with ongoing loss of abilities and resources (Bowd 2003; Cuddy and Fiske 2002; Ellis and Morrison 2005). It is these abilities and resources that are perceived as crucial to acquiring and preserving self-esteem in youth and middle-aged individuals. As a result, these age groups might perceive the older adults as a threat, since they serve as potent reminders of the transitory nature of these attributes. Thus, the threat of loss of these attributes might trigger death anxiety (Martens et al. 2005).[19]

This discrimination against elderly patients is not limited to research; it is observed in the clinic too. Older patients are undertreated when compared to younger patients. For instance, based on clinical vignettes, Protière et al showed that physicians recommend chemotherapy for breast cancer in 99% of cases among people 55 years old, but only 60.4% among people 76 years old whose clinical situations are the same. Moreover, 71% of physicians justified their decisions based on tumor characteristics,

---

[19] Origins of Ageism at the Individual Level
https://link.springer.com/chapter/10.1007/978-3-319-73820-8_4

whereas only 14% based it on the patient's age[20]. Similarly, a UK survey showed that the intensity of cancer treatment is influenced by age in 49% of early-stage cases and 51% of advanced-stage cases[21]. In comparison, comorbidities influence only 37% of recommendations in the early stages and 31% in the advanced stages. Another recent study showed that mortality increases with age among women with breast cancer, and the authors suggest that undertreatment can explain this observation.[22] Indeed, young and old patients are not evenly treated; in the case of breast cancer

[20] Protière C, Viens P, Rousseau F, Moatti JP. Prescribers' attitudes toward elderly breast cancer patients. Discrimination or empathy? Crit Rev Oncol Hematol. 2010;75(2):138–150. [PubMed] [Google Scholar]

[21] Department of Health Pharmaceutical Oncology Initiative . The Impact of Patient Age on Clinical Decision-Making in Oncology. London, UK: Department of Health; 2012. [Google Scholar

[22] van de Water W, Markopoulos C, van de Velde CJ, et al. Association between age at diagnosis and disease-specific mortality among postmenopausal women with hormone receptor-positive breast cancer. JAMA. 2012;307(6):590–597. [PubMed] [Google Scholar]

treatment, older patients have a lower probability of receiving standard care.[23] [24]

Cases to support Part I.

Jury Awards Former Times Sports Columnist $15.4 Million

A Los Angeles jury has awarded T.J. Simers $15.4 million in damages against The Los Angeles Times for discrimination against him because of his age and disability. It was the second time a jury had considered whether Simers should receive damages related to his claim that after 22 years at The Times he was demoted from columnist to writer in 2013 when he developed health problems. One of Simers' attorneys said that, with

---

[23] 19. Markopoulos C, van de Water W. Older patients with breast cancer: is there bias in the treatment they receive? Their Adv Med Oncol. 2012;4(6):321–327. [PMC free article] [PubMed] [Google Scholar]

[24] Ageism and its clinical impact in oncogeriatry: state of knowledge and therapeutic leads

https://www.ncbi.nlm.nih.gov/pmc/articles/PMC4317143/

interest, the publisher will owe $22 million to Simers and his wife.[25]

Google Settles Age-Discrimination Lawsuit For $11 Million

Google has agreed to pay $11 million to end a class-action lawsuit involving 227 people accusing the company of systemically discriminating against job applicants who were over the age of 40. Under the final settlement agreement, presented to a federal judge July 19, plaintiffs will collect an estimated $35,000 each. Under the settlement, parent company Alphabet Inc. must train employees and managers about age bias, create a committee on age diversity in recruiting, and make sure complaints are adequately investigated. [26]

---

[25] *Jury awards former Times sports columnist $15.4 million - Los Angeles Times*. (n.d.). Retrieved February 8, 2021, from
https://www.latimes.com/california/story/2019-08-19/jury-awards-tj-simers-former-times-sports-columnist-15-4-million
[26] *Deja Vu: Google Settles Age Discrimination Lawsuit For $11 Million*. (n.d.). Retrieved February 8, 2021, from

Ageism at Work: The Discrimination No One Talks About

Many not-so-young yet highly talented and richly experienced people often struggle in the Indian job market that is oversupplied with young talent. In an age where the corporate workforce is largely composed of young Millennials, it is often difficult for those belonging to Generation X or the Baby Boomers to feel equally valued and respected. Employers often display negative attitudes towards older workers even if they are not necessarily less healthy or productive than their younger counterparts. Older employees are often overlooked when it comes to new career opportunities and learning and development programs. [27]

---

https://www.forbes.com/sites/patriciagbarnes/2019/07/2 0/deja-vu-google-settles-age-discrimination-lawsuit-for-11-million/?sh=70aeb34971f1

[27] *Is Age an Issue in Indian Workplaces in India?* (n.d.). Retrieved February 8, 2021, from https://www.entrepreneur.com/article/333315

Ageism Is Thriving, So What Are Companies Doing About It?

From not even getting past the first interview to being segregated into niche roles, older workers are still facing discrimination. Some companies are trying to fix that. Companies looking to hire older workers need to be prepared to adjust how they think about getting work done and the types of benefits they offer to attract older workers, such as offering returnships to experienced professionals after time off for child or elder care.[28]

Viewpoint: The Next #MeToo Movement - Older Women Confront Ageism

According to a 2018 AARP report, 64 percent of women say they've been the target of or witnessed age discrimination. It's estimated that only 3 percent of older workers have ever made an official complaint to a supervisor, human resource person, or another

---

[28]Lydia, D. (n.d.). *Ageism is thriving, so what are companies doing about it?* Retrieved February 8, 2021,
from https://www.fastcompany.com/90325055/ageism-is-thriving-so-what-are-companies-doing-about-it

---

organization or government agency. Similar to the shame women felt about sexual harassment prior to the #MeToo movement, many professional women remain silent when subjected to ageist behavior in the workplace. They choose silence, afraid to complain and draw attention to their age for fear they'll lose their jobs. [29]

Survey: Most Older Americans Face Age Discrimination in the Workplace

Fifty-eight percent of Americans age 50 and older say older workers face discrimination in the workplace, and 75 percent consider their own age to be a detriment when looking for a job, according to a survey conducted by The Associated Press-NORC Center for Public Affairs Research. Additionally, among workers aged 50 and older, about a fifth think they have been passed over for

---

[29]Marcus, B. (n.d.). *The next #MeToo movement: Older women confront ageism - Chicago Tribune.*
Retrieved February 8, 2021, from
https://www.chicagotribune.com/opinion/comment
ary/ct-perspec-
metoo-ageism-older-women-discrimination-0321-
20190320-story.html

promotion or raises due to their age. Only 6 percent of older adults say their age is an advantage. [30]

Is Age a Part of Your Inclusion Strategy?

People are living longer, and there are more older people in the workforce and looking for work. The time is ripe for organizations to make age part of their diversity and inclusion strategies, noted panelists at The Future of Work for All Generations conference that AARP recently hosted in Washington, D.C. "You do have to retire the word 'retirement,' " said Julio Portalatin, vice chairman of global professional services firm Marsh & McLennan in New York City. "It is about different stages [of work and life] now … and our ability to reskill at those points".[31]

---

[30]Young, E. (n.d.). *Most Older Americans Face Age Discrimination in the Workplace, New Survey Finds—Working Longer*. Retrieved February 8, 2021, from https://workinglongerstudy.org/most-older americans-face-age-discrimination-in-the-workplace%2C-new-survey-finds/
[31] WESTERN AIR LINES, INC., Petitioner, v. Charles G. CRISWELL et al. | Supreme Court | US Law | LII / Legal Information Institute. (n.d.). Retrieved February 8, 2021, from https://www.law.cornell.edu/supremecourt/text/472/400

Influence on Social standards

When we try to understand this social issue, it is important to understand the implications of age- based bias, on the society. It is not a rare concept that the people follow rules and form conventions, on the basis of what is widely popular in the community of which they are a part and form social standards for the society at large. These standards gradually gain momentum. It is not necessary that what gains the approval of the majority is always right. Such "conventionally formed behavior", may or may not be right. But no one person, stops or can stop the force of a social standard, unless such wrongful behavior is corrected.

Social norms, the informal rules that govern behavior in groups and societies, have been extensively studied in the social sciences. Anthropologists have described how social norms function in different cultures (Geertz 1973), sociologists have focused on their social functions and how they motivate people to act (Durkheim 1895 [1982], 1950 [1957]; Parsons 1937; Parsons & Shils 1951; James Coleman 1990; Hechter & Opp 2001), and economists have explored how adherence to norms influences market behavior (Akerlof 1976; Young 1998a). More recently, also legal scholars have touted social norms as efficient alternatives to legal rules, as they may internalize negative externalities and provide signaling mechanisms at little or no cost (Ellickson 1991; Posner 2000).[32]

Cultural beliefs shape social norms and values surrounding the ageing process and the role of older people. These beliefs about aging are not static -they shift and change as society evolves. Like other social groups such as women or African Americans, myths have emerged and, over time, have become part of the social fabric. These ageing myths which form the basis for stereotypes create a limited social perspective on older people and as a consequence older people are thought of and treated as if they are all the same. However these myths are socially constructed which means they can be

---

[32] *Social Norms (Stanford Encyclopedia of Philosophy/Winter 2018 Edition)*. (n.d.). Retrieved February 8, 2021, from https://plato.stanford.edu/archives/win2018/entries/social-norms/

challenged. Social work values stress the importance of social justice for those who are vulnerable and oppressed and older adults are among those groups that can be at risk. Thus, it is important to confront the ageing myths that we have been socialised to believe because these myths and stereotypes have a direct negative impact on older people in terms of receiving services or opportunities within society, becoming more self-aware about how these ideas are limiting our conception of older people can facilitate change.[33]

---

[33] *Aging and Ageism: Cultural Influences Learning Objectives*. (n.d.). Retrieved February 8, 2021, from https://us.sagepub.com/sites/default/files/upm-assets/90251_book_item_90251.pdf

Examples- areas where age is a criterion and thus a restraint-Retirement, Marriage, Political qualification, Professions

As we see, due to the social standards being formed, age has become a criterion for numerous institutions, like marriage, the legal age to marry in most countries is 18 years. Globally, the average legal age of marriage for boys is 17 and 16 for girls but many countries permit them, particularly girls, to marry much younger.[34] Many professions, as we have seen earlier, have age as a criterion, notifying the belief of directly proportional relation between age and years of experience, which makes them deemed "fit" or "qualified" enough for the job.

---

[34] *World minimum marriage age: Chart shows the lowest age you can legally get married around the world | The Independent | The Independent.* (n.d.). Retrieved February 8, 2021, from https://www.independent.co.uk/news/world/lowest-age-you-can-legally-get-married-around-world-10415517.html

In the EU Member States, the most general retirement age is 65 years. Spain, Germany and France are about to raise their retirement age from 65 to 67 years, while the goal is 68 years in Britain and Ireland. Increasingly, the retirement age is being linked to life expectancy. In addition to Finland this mechanism is available in Cyprus, Denmark, Estonia, Greece, Italy, the Netherlands, Portugal and Slovakia. Also, in Britain, after mechanical increases, the retirement age will rise taking life expectancy into account.[35] [36]

---

[35] *Retirement Ages - Finnish Centre for Pensions*. (n.d.). Retrieved February 8, 2021, from https://www.etk.fi/en/work-and-pensions-abroad/international-comparisons/retirement-ages/
[36] Bratt, C., Abrams, D., Swift, H. J., Vauclair, C. M., & Marques, S. (2018). Perceived age discrimination across age in Europe: From an ageing society to a society for all ages. *Developmental Psychology, 54*(1), 167–180. https://doi.org/10.1037/dev0000398

Other countries	Men / Women	Retirement age or men/women
Australia	58 years; 66 years*	60 years (2024); 67 years (2023)*
Canada (CA)	65 years	–
Iceland (IS)	67 years	
Japan (JP)	63 years / 61 years; 65*	65 years (2025) / 65 years (2030); –
Norway (NO)	62–75 years;67 years*	–

Russia (RU)	60 years and 6 months / 55 years and 6 months	65 years (2028); 60 (2028)
Switzerland (CH)	65 years / 64 years	–
USA (US)	66 years	67 years (2027)

As we can see, the retirement age is set by most countries, to determine whether a person is "fit enough" to work in the organization. It is important to understand that age is used by many organizations to assess the productivity and efficiency of an individual and thus to predict the worth of an individual, once he/she/they reach a certain age.

Comparative Analysis of impact in various countries - Answering "Where?"

From the previous sections we have seen how various aspects of human life are impacted by ageism. Now to have a well-rounded analysis, we have to examine the impact in different countries. For this purpose, the following study can be considered as useful.[37]

Recent data from 20,788 adults aged 16–64 from 30 countries around the world revealed that 23% of the respondents agreed that older people are treated unfairly and that globally 60% of respondents reported that older adults are not well respected (Hall et al. 2019). This chimes with the World Health Organizations' analysis of the World Values Survey data from 83,034 adults from 57 countries (conducted between 2010 and 2014), which also found that 60% of participants agreed there is a lack

---

[37] Bratt, C., Abrams, D., Swift, H. J., Vauclair, C. M., & Marques, S. (2018). Perceived age discrimination across age in Europe: From an ageing society to a society for all ages. *Developmental Psychology*, *54*(1), 167–180. https://doi.org/10.1037/dev0000398

of respect afforded to older people (Officer et al. 2016). Thus, there seems to be an agreement and an expectation among these respondents that ageism, in the form of lack of respect and being treated unfairly, will emerge in later life.[38]

The study shows how adults across the globe face ageism. Now we will take a look at a few of the countries in detail.

Starting from India, where are no legal remedies specifically catered to age discrimination. But, the Constitution of India provides fundamental rights, with the help of common laws, it can be used for remedies.
"(1) The State shall not discriminate against any citizen on grounds only of religion, race, caste, sex, place of birth or any of them.

---

[38] Swift, H. J., Abrams, D., & Lamont, R. A. (2019). Ageism Around the World. In *Encyclopedia of Gerontology and Population Aging* (pp. 1–12). Springer International Publishing. https://doi.org/10.1007/978-3-319-69892-2_586-1

(2) No citizen shall, on grounds only of religion, race, caste, sex, place of birth or any of them, be subject to any disability, liability, restriction or condition with regard to—

(a) access to shops, public restaurants, hotels and places of public entertainment; or

(b) the use of wells, tanks, bathing ghats, roads and places of public resort maintained wholly or partly out of State funds or dedicated to the use of the general public."[39]

Coming to U.S.A, The Age Discrimination in Employment Act (ADEA) forbids age discrimination against people who are age 40 or older. It does not protect workers under the age of 40, although some states have laws that protect younger workers from age discrimination. It is not illegal for an employer or other

---

[39]*Constitution of India.* (n.d.). Retrieved February 8, 2021, from
https://www.constitutionofindia.net/constitution_of_indi a/fundamental_rights/articles/Article 15

covered entity to favor an older worker over a younger one, even if both workers are age 40 or older.[40]

To understand more about this Act mentioned above, the Age Discrimination Act of 1975 prohibits discrimination on the basis of age in programs and activities receiving federal financial assistance. The Act, which applies to all ages, permits the use of certain age distinctions and factors other than age that meet the Act's requirements. The Age Discrimination Act is enforced by the Civil Rights Center. The Age Discrimination in Employment Act of 1967 (ADEA) protects certain applicants and employees 40 years of age and older from discrimination on the basis of age in hiring, promotion, discharge, compensation, or terms, conditions or privileges of employment. The ADEA is enforced by the Equal Employment Opportunity Commission.[41]

---

[40] *Age Discrimination | U.S. Equal Employment Opportunity Commission.* (n.d.). Retrieved February 8, 2021, from https://www.eeoc.gov/age-discrimination
[41] *Age Discrimination | U.S. Department of Labor.* (n.d.). Retrieved February 8, 2021, from https://www.dol.gov/general/topic/discrimination/agedisc

Coming to China, China doesn't have laws prohibiting discrimination based on age, and age discrimination reportedly starts younger than in the United States. Many job postings in China seek applicants younger than 35 years old. (The ADEA's protections do not apply until 40 years old.)[42]

Next country to examine is Russia. Age discrimination in employment is explicitly prohibited by the Russian Labor Code. Certain age-based variations in employment conditions, limitations, preferences, etc. are established by the Labor Code or other federal laws in view of the job requirements and workplace conditions.[43]

The current retirement age in Russia is 60 for men and 55 for women. However, on October 03, 2018, the Russian

---

[42]

[43] *Russia — age discrimination.* (n.d.). Retrieved February 8, 2021, from http://www.agediscrimination.info/international-age-discrimination/russia

---

President signed the Law which will come into effect on January 01, 2019, increasing the retirement ages. Under the Law, the retirement age will be increased every year, until it reaches 65 for men and 63 for women. Generally, an employer cannot force an employee to retire upon reaching a certain age or to move to another position. On October 03, 2018 the Russian President signed the Law on liability for unjustified denial in employment and dismissal of a person of pre-retirement age (i.e. 5 years prior to reaching the retirement age) which comes into force on October 14, 2018 and is based on literal wording of the law, i.e. dismissal of a person of pre- retirement age can be recognized as unjustified, if such person proves that his/her dismissal is connected with his/her age. [44]

Labor Code of the Russian Federation of 31 December 2001 (Federal Law No. 197-FZ of 2001) states that-: [45]

---

[44] *Russia — age discrimination.* (n.d.). Retrieved February 8, 2021, from http://www.agediscrimination.info/international-age-discrimination/russi

[45] *Russian Federation. LABOR CODE OF THE RUSSIAN FEDERATION OF 31 DECEMBER 2001.* (n.d.). Retrieved February 8, 2021, from

Article 2. Main principles of legal regulation of labor relations and other relations directly linked to them

- prohibition of forced labor and discrimination in the sphere of labor;
- equality of employees' rights and opportunities.

Article 3. Prohibition of discrimination in the sphere of labor

Everyone shall have equal opportunities to realize his/her labor rights. No one can be constrained in his/her labor rights and freedoms or get any advantages irrespective of sex, race, color of skin, nationality, language, origins, property, social or position status, age, domicile, religious beliefs, political convictions, affiliation or non-affiliation with public associations as well as other factors not relevant to professional qualities of the employee. Establishment of distinctions, exceptions, preferences as well as limitation of employees' rights which are determined by the requirements inherent in a specific

http://www.ilo.org/dyn/natlex/docs/WEBTEXT/60535/65252/E01RUS01.ht#chap62

kind of work as set by federal laws or caused by especial attention of the state to the persons requiring increased social and legal protection shall not be deemed discrimination. The persons considering themselves to be discriminated against in the sphere of labor shall be entitled to petition the federal labor inspectorate bodies and/or courts applying for restoration of their violated rights, compensation of the material loss and redress of the moral damage.[46]

Best possible system in all

By understanding the laws in some of the major countries, it can be concluded that the law enforcement to prevent age discrimination is required, as it provides clear remedies that are available for the victims of age discrimination. But one thing that's significant to note is that in most countries, the recognition is not enough for age discrimination that is suffered by young people. It is important to address that as well. By spreading awareness

---

[46] The same as 45;.

---

through recognition, these victims' voices are heard and such practice could be prohibited right at its budding phase. It is also important to note that the age discrimination laws are restricted to workplace and this priority is set by most countries. But, with our study, we can understand that this bias is found even in the society at large, outside the workplace. To combat this, it is important that governments acknowledge the trauma which will in turn provide confidence to stop this at individual and personal level.

A very important legal maxim to keep in mind here is, Ubi jus ibi remedium. The principle that where one's right is invaded or destroyed, the law gives a remedy to protect it or damages for its loss. Further, where one's right is denied the law affords the remedy of an action for its enforcement. This right to a remedy therefore includes more than is usually meant in English law by the term "remedy", as it includes a right of action. Wherever, therefore, a right exists there is also a remedy. Ashby v White (1703) 14 St Tr 695, 92 ER 126 (or rather the classic judgment of Lord Chief Justice Holt in that case) is usually cited to exemplify the maxim. This principle, which has at all times been considered so valuable, gave occasion to the first invention of that form of action called an action on the case. Such actions played a major part in the development of the law of tort.[47]

As a set of solutions these are the following measures that can be taken up-

1. Acknowledging diversity, in the society as well as in the workforce.

    This practice can be started by the companies who hire employees, they can acknowledge and appreciate the array of experiences that people bring with themselves in the team, which results in innovation, creativity, diversity, and increased productivity, and efficiency.

2. Better law reforms through statutes

    Wherein actions of age discrimination of any kind are explicitly prohibited. Penalties and

---

[47] *Ubi jus ibi remedium - Oxford Reference.* (n.d.). Retrieved February 8, 2021, from https://www.oxfordreference.com/view/10.1093/oi/authority.20110803110448446

offences are clearly stated for contraventions and violations of any kind.

3. Efficient law enforcement

It is important that not only the laws are drafted, but it is made sure that they are enforced by keeping a check through executive and administrative bodies of the government.

4. Statutory authorities to be created

Statutory authorities and administrative tribunals need to be formed that look after strictly the enforcement of the Age discrimination laws. This enables authorities to efficiently look into these issues, speeds up the remedial process and encourages people to opt for judicial remedies, creating a good society at large.

5. Education and awareness

This measure is a reformative way to combat ageism over time. It is important that awareness is spread to everyone about the plight of people who are preys of this discrimination. It is important to kill this evil from its core and wipe such bias from the minds of the people.

To prove with an example, Switzerland has one of the highest employment rates for older workers in the OECD. In 2012, 70.5% of Swiss aged 55-64 were in work, behind Iceland (79.2%), New Zealand (73.9%), Sweden (73.1%) and Norway (70.9%), exceeding the OECD average of 54% by almost 17 percentage points.

As highlighted by the OECD in its 2006 report Live Longer, Work Longer, however, to be effective, laws against age discrimination must be supported by information campaigns and guidelines that encourage best age-management practices at work.[48]

According to the OECD Report of 2014, the key drivers for change in enterprises are the following: [49]

---

[48] Working Better with Age: Switzerland-Assessment and recommendations © OECD Directorate for Employment, Labour and Social Affairs Employment Working Better with Age SWITZERLAND Assessment and main recommendations. (2014).

[49] The same as 48

- Combating age discrimination. Information campaigns are needed to tackle negative attitudes to older people in the workplace.
- Encouraging the social partners to link pay more to experience than to age.
- Involving enterprises as early as possible in the implementation of the Initiative to combat the shortage of skilled workers.
- Stepping up action to inform and advise employers about age management.

This can inspire other countries to do the same to provide support to those who need them by implementing powerful measures.

Case laws to support Part II

In the USA, a number of landmark cases have interpreted the ADEA since its passage. Western Air Lines v. Criswell, 472 U.S. 400, 105 S. Ct. 2743, 86L. Ed. 2d 321 (1985), set out the guidelines for defending an age limit based on the BFOQ exception. Western required flight engineers, who are members of the flight crew but generally do not operate flight controls, to retire at age 60. When this policy was challenged, the airline maintained that the age limit was a BFOQ necessary to ensure safety. The Supreme Court disagreed, and in a unanimous decision announced a two-pronged test to be applied when evaluating a BFOQ based on safety:

(1) whether the age limit is reasonably necessary to the overriding interest in public safety; and (2) whether the employer is justified in applying the age limit to all

Case laws to support Part II

employees rather than deciding each case on an individual basis.[50]

In another case the same year, the Supreme Court found TWA guilty of age discrimination for refusing to transfer pilots to the position of flight engineer after they reached age 60, the Federal Aviation Administration's (FAA's) mandatory retirement age for pilots[51]. TWA had allowed younger pilots who had become disabled to transfer automatically to the position of flight engineer, but did not allow pilots and copilots past the age of 60 to do the same. The Court held that the airline must give the same opportunity to retiring pilots and copilots as it had given to younger disabled pilots. However, the Court denied the pilots' request for double damages, which are allowed in cases of "willful violation" of the ADEA, stating that a violation is willful only if the employer knew that its

---

[50] Western Air Lines v. Criswell, 472 U.S. 400, 105 S. Ct. 2743, 86L. Ed. 2d 321 (1985)
[51] (Trans World Airlines v. Thurston, 469 U.S. 111, 105 S. Ct. 613, 83 L. Ed. 2d 523 [1985])

conduct was prohibited by the ADEA or showed a "reckless disregard" for whether the act applied.[52]

Few other cases to support our research are-:
Air India Vs. Nergesh Meerza and Others (AIR 1981 SC 1829)

The case imposed a challenge on Regulations 46 and 47 of the Air India Employees Service Regulations. With the challenge being posited on the grounds that the aforesaid regulation created a substantial degree of disparity between male (referred to as Air Flight Pursers) and female (Air Hostesses) (and within the Air Hostesses different operational standards dependent on whether one is working for Air India International on the International circuit or Indian Airlines on the domestic circuit) on multitude of grounds such as promotional avenues, differential retirement ages, conditions pertaining to

---

[52] *Age Discrimination - Landmark Discrimination Cases - Pilots, Adea, Flight, and Court - JRank Articles.* (n.d.). Retrieved February 8, 2021, from https://law.jrank.org/pages/4166/Age-Discrimination-Landmark-Discrimination-Cases.html

termination of the Air hostesses services in cases of pregnancy or marriage (retirement age for them was 35 years as opposed to 58 for their "male counterparts" – according to Regulation 46). Furthermore, a more prosaic question was regarding the discretionary powers of the Managing Director who under Regulation 47 could increase the age of retirement as per his own behest. An aspect which is contested by the petitioners as being arbitrary.

Article 16 Of The Constitution of India provides that there is Equality of opportunity in matters of public employment and the Regulation 46 Air India Employees Service Regulations provide that Retiring Age: Subject to the provisions of sub-regulation (ii) hereof an employee shall retire from the service of the Corporation upon attaining the age of 58 years, except in the following cases when he/she shall retire earlier: (c) An Air Hostess, upon attaining the age of 35 years or on marriage if it takes place within four years of service or on first pregnancy, whichever occurs earlier.[53]

Indian Council Of Legal Aid & Advice v. Bar Council Of India on 17 January, 1995 (citations: 1995 AIR 691, 1995 SCC (1) 732)

> "A person who has completed the age of 45 years on the date on which he submits his application for his enrolment as an advocate to the State Bar Council shall not be enrolled as an advocate."[54]

The Supreme Court has upheld verdicts of various High Courts quashing a rule framed by several State Bar Councils fixing the upper age limit of 45 years for enrolment as an advocate.[55] Setting an example that age

---

[53] *Air India Etc. Etc vs Nergesh Meerza & Ors. Etc. Etc on 28 August, 1981.* (n.d.). Retrieved February 8, 2021,
[54] *Indian Council Of Legal Aid & Advice Vs. Bar Council Of India on 17 January, 1995 - Legitquest.* (n.d.). Retrieved February 8, 2021, from https://www.legitquest.com/case/indian-council-of-legal-aid-advice-v-bar-council-of-india/ee2
[55] The same as 54;.

discrimination violates basic human rights of an individual.

Reasons explained

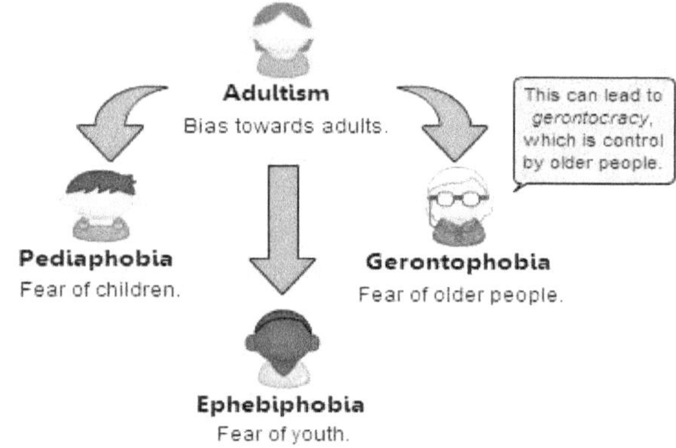

[56](Picture source - Freechild Organisation)

As we have already discussed in the previous section about the causes of ageism, it is important to identify the reasons not only from the scientific and theoretical point of view but also to understand the social and practical reasons, to allow a more realistic approach. This will help in combating it more efficiently.

---

[56] *Understanding the Causes of Age Discrimination – Freechild Institute*. (n.d.). Retrieved February 8, 2021, from https://freechild.org/2016/01/07/age-discrimination/

Reasons are-:

1. Fear of competition and Survival

2. Arrogance of the modern world

3. Lack of association with diverse people

4. Resistance to adjustment and compromise

5. Rigid behavior

6. Presumptions

7. Generality added to entire section by one bad experience

8. Compartmentalization and categorization

Personal opinions

To further explain these reasons, we take them one by one. Firstly, the fear of competition and survival, in this world, makes people act in ways that cannot truly define them. The world has always been a very competitive place to be. Everyone is here for survival. In the primitive times, it was the survival of the fittest, where fittest is the person judged physically. But now humans have evolved to different versions of "survival of the fittest" where people are judged based on their mental capacity, their efficiency, their earnings and other materialistic things. This fear makes them belittle others to reduce their competition and come out as superior.

Secondly, the world is adapting to modernization, it is good in many aspects but one of the downsides of modernization is arrogance, which people start inculcating with their modern thoughts. They challenge everything in the world with practicality and their rational thinking. Anything can survive only if it can survive the practical approach of modern people. They are critical and constructive about everything ranging from religion to customs, traditions and rituals.

Thirdly, this mentality has become widespread because less and less people have spent time and have associated less with age- varied sections of people in their life. The only generation that is okay according to them is theirs, dismissing the older and the younger. Fourthly, in today's times, it's a common observation that people are resistant to change. As changes bring difficulties and newer adjustments. Thus, people try to stay in the comfort zones, and try as much to not evolve so that it does not give them difficulties. The lack of compromise when it comes to diverse people, makes it difficult to bring harmony in the society at large.

Fifthly, this is nothing but a sign of rigid behavior, which makes it absolutely impossible to resolve differences, see everyone as an equal and provide people with equal and respectful opportunities. Society becomes less harmonious and peaceful. Sixthly, there are presumptions made by people when it comes to a person belonging to a certain group. There are attributes that are associated with sections of different ages, as we saw in the previous sections. This presumptuous nature makes it more difficult. Seventhly, generality added to the entire section by one bad experience, this is self-explanatory. Just because there was one bad experience or event that happened with one person of a particular group, it is generally added as a quality for all belonging to that group. Forgiveness can help in these situations. Finally, compartmentalization. We, as a society have learned a habit of putting people in boxes and categories to learn and to make it easy for ourselves. Whatever the reason, it does not help and is rather counterproductive. These categories are based on materialistic features like money, beauty, height, weight, and age. All this drowns and overpowers what really matters in life and which is nature and kindness.

Conclusion

There are many issues the world is facing. Issues that are far more magnanimous and far more catastrophic. Individuals are facing their own issues in their own lives and realizing how unstable life is and how different lives are of each and everyone. But somehow, it all comes to a standstill. When nature runs its course, proving to humanity how powerful it is. Humanity then realizes its strength. The only way to face these issues is to stand together against the problem. Like every problem in the world, be it a war, a pandemic, or a financial crisis or racism, every problem started with an origin. An origin which could have prevented. Had it been stopped at its origin, the damage that these problems have created, could have been avoided.

When slavery and racism started initially, no one could have realized how damaging it is. It took slavery to become an inhuman custom, that voice was raised against it only to abolish it. Had there been education and prevention at the start, damage wouldn't have taken place.

It was only after the first world war, that the world realized that even if machines can win battles, in the end it's humanity that loses irrespective of which side wins. This paper is a step to make the readers realize how right now is the time which is the origin of a problem that people in the entire world face silently. The damage to one's mental health can be avoided, just by taking a few steps now, which is to educate. What has happened in the past cannot be changed but the new changes, if adopted, can help people, to defeat discrimination and oppression of one kind and of all kinds.

Bibliography:

Abhyu. (2017). *A Case Note Examining the First de-Facto Case of Sexual Discrimination at the Work Place: Air India v Nergesh Meerza & Ors 1981 AIR 1829 - iPleaders*. IPleaders. https://blog.ipleaders.in/a-case-note-examining-the-first-de-facto-case-of-sexual-discrimination-at-the-work-place/

Akerlof, G. (1976). The economics of caste and of the rat race and other woeful tales. *Quarterly Journal of Economics*, *90*(4), 599–617. https://doi.org/10.2307/1885324

Akerlof, G. (1976). The economics of caste and of the rat race and other woeful tales. *Quarterly Journal of Economics*, *90*(4), 599–617. https://doi.org/10.2307/1885324

Alexander, J. M. K. (2000). Evolutionary explanations of distributive justice. *Philosophy of Science*, *67*(3), 490–516. https://doi.org/10.1086/392792

Alexander, J. M. K. (2000). Evolutionary explanations of distributive justice. *Philosophy of Science*, *67*(3), 490–516. https://doi.org/10.1086/392792

Alexander, J. M. (2007). The structural evolution of morality. In *The Structural Evolution of Morality*. Cambridge University Press. https://doi.org/10.1017/CBO9780511550997

Alexander, J. M. (2007). The structural evolution of morality. In *The Structural Evolution of Morality*. Cambridge University Press. https://doi.org/10.1017/CBO9780511550997

ALRUD. (2018). *Russia — age discrimination*. http://www.agediscrimination.info/international-age-discrimination/russia

ALRUD. (n.d.). *Russia — age discrimination*. Retrieved February 8, 2021, from http://www.agediscrimination.info/international-age-discrimination/russia

Altbach, P. G., De, H., Ang, N., Stanfield, D., & Ergin, H. (2020). *Postpandemic Outlook: Bleakest for the Poorest Singapore: An Early and Measured Response Crisis upon Crisis: COVID-19 and Student Refugees*. www.internationalhighereducation.

ANDREONI, J., & S BERNHEIM, D. (2009). Social Image and the 50-50 Norm: A Theoretical and Experimental Analysis of Audience Effects. *Econometrica, 77*(5), 1607–1636. https://doi.org/10.3982/ecta7384

Arrow, K. J. (1971). A utilitarian approach to the concept of equality in public expenditures. *Quarterly Journal of Economics, 85*(3), 409–415. https://doi.org/10.2307/1885930

Arrow, K. J. (1971). A utilitarian approach to the concept of equality in public expenditures. *Quarterly Journal of Economics, 85*(3), 409–415. https://doi.org/10.2307/1885930

Axelrod, R. (1986). An evolutionary approach to norms. *American Political Science Review, 80*(4), 1095–1111. https://doi.org/10.1017/S0003055400185016

Axelrod, R. (1986). An evolutionary approach to norms. *American Political Science Review, 80*(4), 1095–1111. https://doi.org/10.1017/S0003055400185016

Barnes, P. (2019). *Deja Vu: Google Settles Age Discrimination Lawsuit For $11 Million*. https://www.forbes.com/sites/patriciagbarnes/2019

/07/20/deja-vu-google-settles-age-discrimination-lawsuit-for-11-million/?sh=70aeb34971f1

Barnes, P. (n.d.). *Deja Vu: Google Settles Age Discrimination Lawsuit For $11 Million*. Retrieved February 8, 2021, from https://www.forbes.com/sites/patriciagbarnes/2019/07/20/deja-vu-google-settles-age-discrimination-lawsuit-for-11-million/#8ec5c1a71f1e

Bass, R. V. . G. J. W. (2004). *ERIC - EJ724880 - Educare and Educere: Is a Balance Possible in the Educational System?, Educational Forum, The, 2004*. Educational Forum, The, V68 N2 P161-168 Win . https://eric.ed.gov/?id=EJ724880

Battigalli, P., & Dufwenberg, M. (2009). Dynamic psychological games. *Journal of Economic Theory*, *144*(1), 1–35. https://doi.org/10.1016/j.jet.2008.01.004

Battigalli, P., & Dufwenberg, M. (2009). Dynamic psychological games. *Journal of Economic Theory*, *144*(1), 1–35. https://doi.org/10.1016/j.jet.2008.01.004

Battigalli, P., & Dufwenberg, M. (2007). Guilt in games. *American Economic Review*, *97*(2), 170–176. https://doi.org/10.1257/aer.97.2.170

Battigalli, P., & Dufwenberg, M. (2007). Guilt in games. *American Economic Review*, *97*(2), 170–176. https://doi.org/10.1257/aer.97.2.170

Bénabou, R., & Tirole, J. (2006). Incentives and prosocial behavior. *American Economic Review*, *96*(5), 1652–1678. https://doi.org/10.1257/aer.96.5.1652

Bénabou, R., & Tirole, J. (2006). Incentives and prosocial behavior. *American Economic Review*,

96(5), 1652–1678.
https://doi.org/10.1257/aer.96.5.1652

Bicchieri, C. (2002). Covenants without swords: Group identity, norms, and communication in social dilemmas. In *Rationality and Society* (Vol. 14, Issue 2, pp. 192–228). SAGE Publications Ltd. https://doi.org/10.1177/1043463102014002003

Bicchieri, C. (2002). Covenants without swords: Group identity, norms, and communication in social dilemmas. In *Rationality and Society* (Vol. 14, Issue 2, pp. 192–228). SAGE Publications Ltd. https://doi.org/10.1177/1043463102014002003

Bicchieri, C. (2017). Norms in the wild: How to diagnose, measure, and change social norms. In *Norms in the Wild: How to Diagnose, Measure, and Change Social Norms*. Oxford University Press. https://doi.org/10.1093/acprof:oso/9780190622046.001.0001

Bicchieri, C. (2017). Norms in the wild: How to diagnose, measure, and change social norms. In *Norms in the Wild: How to Diagnose, Measure, and Change Social Norms*. Oxford University Press. https://doi.org/10.1093/acprof:oso/9780190622046.001.0001

Bicchieri, C. (1990). Norms of Cooperation. *Ethics, 100*(4), 838–861. https://doi.org/10.1086/293237

Bicchieri, C. (1990). Norms of Cooperation. *Ethics, 100*(4), 838–861. https://doi.org/10.1086/293237

Bicchieri, C. (2005). The grammar of society: The nature and dynamics of social norms. In *The Grammar of Society: The Nature and Dynamics of*

Social Norms. Cambridge University Press.
https://doi.org/10.1017/CBO9780511616037
Bicchieri, C. (2005). The grammar of society: The
nature and dynamics of social norms. In *The
Grammar of Society: The Nature and Dynamics of
Social Norms*. Cambridge University Press.
https://doi.org/10.1017/CBO9780511616037
Bicchieri, C. R. M. and A. S. (2011). *Social Norms
(Stanford Encyclopedia of Philosophy)*.
https://plato.stanford.edu/entries/social-norms/
Bicchieri, C., & Chavez, A. (2010). Behaving as
expected: Public information and fairness norms.
Journal of Behavioral Decision Making, 23(2),
161–178. https://doi.org/10.1002/bdm.648
Bicchieri, C., & Chavez, A. (2010). Behaving as
expected: Public information and fairness norms.
Journal of Behavioral Decision Making, 23(2),
161–178. https://doi.org/10.1002/bdm.648
Bicchieri, C., Duffy, J., & Tolle, G. (2004). Trust among
strangers. *Philosophy of Science, 71*(3), 286–319.
https://doi.org/10.1086/381411
Bicchieri, C., Duffy, J., & Tolle, G. (2004). Trust among
strangers. *Philosophy of Science, 71*(3), 286–319.
https://doi.org/10.1086/381411
Bicchieri, C., & Fukui, Y. (1999). The Great Illusion:
Ignorance, Informational Cascades, and the
Persistence of Unpopular Norms. *Business Ethics
Quarterly, 9*(1), 127–155.
https://doi.org/10.2307/3857639
Bicchieri, C., & Fukui, Y. (1999). The Great Illusion:
Ignorance, Informational Cascades, and the
Persistence of Unpopular Norms. *Business Ethics*

Quarterly, 9(1), 127–155.
https://doi.org/10.2307/3857639

Bicchieri, C., & Lev-on, A. (2007). Computer-mediated communication and cooperation in social dilemmas: An experimental analysis. *Politics, Philosophy & Economics, 6*(2), 139–168. https://doi.org/10.1177/1470594X07077267

Bicchieri, C., & Lev-on, A. (2007). Computer-mediated communication and cooperation in social dilemmas: An experimental analysis. *Politics, Philosophy & Economics, 6*(2), 139–168. https://doi.org/10.1177/1470594X07077267

Bicchieri, C., & Sontuoso, A. (2015). I cannot cheat on you after we talk. In *The Prisoner's Dilemma* (pp. 101–114). Cambridge University Press. https://doi.org/10.1017/CBO9781107360174.007

Bicchieri, C., & Sontuoso, A. (2015). I cannot cheat on you after we talk. In *The Prisoner's Dilemma* (pp. 101–114). Cambridge University Press. https://doi.org/10.1017/CBO9781107360174.007

Bicchieri, C., & Xiao, E. (2009). Do the right thing: But only if others do so. *Journal of Behavioral Decision Making, 22*(2), 191–208. https://doi.org/10.1002/bdm.621

Bicchieri, C., & Xiao, E. (2009). Do the right thing: But only if others do so. *Journal of Behavioral Decision Making, 22*(2), 191–208. https://doi.org/10.1002/bdm.621

Binmore, K. (2010). Social norms or social preferences? *Mind and Society, 9*(2), 139–157. https://doi.org/10.1007/s11299-010-0073-2

Binmore, K. (2010). Social norms or social preferences? *Mind and Society*, *9*(2), 139–157. https://doi.org/10.1007/s11299-010-0073-2

Binmore, K. G., & Samuelson, L. (1992). Evolutionary stability in repeated games played by finite automata. *Journal of Economic Theory*, *57*(2), 278–305. https://doi.org/10.1016/0022-0531(92)90037-I

Binmore, K. G., & Samuelson, L. (1992). Evolutionary stability in repeated games played by finite automata. *Journal of Economic Theory*, *57*(2), 278–305. https://doi.org/10.1016/0022-0531(92)90037-I

Bolton, G. E., & Ockenfels, A. (2000). ERC: A theory of equity, reciprocity, and competition. *American Economic Review*, *90*(1), 166–193. https://doi.org/10.1257/aer.90.1.166

Bolton, G. E., & Ockenfels, A. (2000). ERC: A theory of equity, reciprocity, and competition. *American Economic Review*, *90*(1), 166–193. https://doi.org/10.1257/aer.90.1.166

Bornstein, G., & Ben-Yossef, M. (1994). Cooperation in Intergroup and Single-Group Social Dilemmas. *Journal of Experimental Social Psychology*, *30*(1), 52–67. https://doi.org/10.1006/jesp.1994.1003

Bornstein, G., & Ben-Yossef, M. (1994). Cooperation in Intergroup and Single-Group Social Dilemmas. *Journal of Experimental Social Psychology*, *30*(1), 52–67. https://doi.org/10.1006/jesp.1994.1003

Bratt, C., Abrams, D., Swift, H. J., Vauclair, C. M., & Marques, S. (2018). Perceived age discrimination across age in Europe: From an ageing society to a society for all ages. *Developmental Psychology*,

54(1), 167–180.
https://doi.org/10.1037/dev0000398

Bratt, C., Abrams, D., Swift, H. J., Vauclair, C. M., & Marques, S. (2018). Perceived age discrimination across age in Europe: From an ageing society to a society for all ages. *Developmental Psychology*, *54*(1), 167–180.
https://doi.org/10.1037/dev0000398

Brennan, G., Eriksson, L., Goodin, R. E., & Southwood, N. (2013). Explaining Norms. In *Explaining Norms*. Oxford University Press.
https://doi.org/10.1093/acprof:oso/9780199654680.001.0001

Brennan, G., Eriksson, L., Goodin, R. E., & Southwood, N. (2013). Explaining Norms. In *Explaining Norms*. Oxford University Press.
https://doi.org/10.1093/acprof:oso/9780199654680.001.0001

Brewer, M. B. (1979). In-group bias in the minimal intergroup situation: A cognitive-motivational analysis. *Psychological Bulletin*, *86*(2), 307–324.
https://doi.org/10.1037/0033-2909.86.2.307

Brewer, M. B. (1979). In-group bias in the minimal intergroup situation: A cognitive-motivational analysis. *Psychological Bulletin*, *86*(2), 307–324.
https://doi.org/10.1037/0033-2909.86.2.307

Brewer, M. B. (1991). The Social Self: On Being the Same and Different at the Same Time. *Personality and Social Psychology Bulletin*, *17*(5), 475–482.
https://doi.org/10.1177/0146167291175001

Brewer, M. B. (1991). The Social Self: On Being the Same and Different at the Same Time. *Personality*

and Social Psychology Bulletin, *17*(5), 475–482.
https://doi.org/10.1177/0146167291175001

Butler, R. N. (2009). Combating ageism. In *International Psychogeriatrics* (Vol. 21, Issue 2, p. 211). Cambridge University Press. https://doi.org/10.1017/S104161020800731X

Cappelen, A. W., Hole, A. D., Sørensen, E., & Tungodden, B. (2007). The pluralism of fairness ideals: An experimental approach. *American Economic Review*, *97*(3), 818–827. https://doi.org/10.1257/aer.97.3.818

Cappelen, A. W., Hole, A. D., Sørensen, E., & Tungodden, B. (2007). The pluralism of fairness ideals: An experimental approach. *American Economic Review*, *97*(3), 818–827. https://doi.org/10.1257/aer.97.3.818

Charness, G., & Rabin, M. (2002). Understanding social preferences with simple tests. *Quarterly Journal of Economics*, *117*(3), 817–869. https://doi.org/10.1162/003355302760193904

Charness, G., & Rabin, M. (2002). Understanding social preferences with simple tests. *Quarterly Journal of Economics*, *117*(3), 817–869. https://doi.org/10.1162/003355302760193904

Chavez, A. K., & Bicchieri, C. (2013). Third-party sanctioning and compensation behavior: Findings from the ultimatum game. *Journal of Economic Psychology*, *39*, 268–277. https://doi.org/10.1016/j.joep.2013.09.004

Chavez, A. K., & Bicchieri, C. (2013). Third-party sanctioning and compensation behavior: Findings from the ultimatum game. *Journal of Economic*

Psychology, 39, 268–277.
https://doi.org/10.1016/j.joep.2013.09.004
Cialdini, R. B., & Goldstein, N. J. (2004). Social influence: Compliance and conformity. *Annual Review of Psychology, 55*, 591–621. https://doi.org/10.1146/annurev.psych.55.090902.142015
Cialdini, R. B., & Goldstein, N. J. (2004). Social influence: Compliance and conformity. *Annual Review of Psychology, 55*, 591–621. https://doi.org/10.1146/annurev.psych.55.090902.142015
Cialdini, R. B., Kallgren, C. A., & Reno, R. R. (1991). A Focus Theory of Normative Conduct: A Theoretical Refinement and Reevaluation of the Role of Norms in Human Behavior. *Advances in Experimental Social Psychology, 24*(C), 201–234. https://doi.org/10.1016/S0065-2601(08)60330-5
Cialdini, R. B., Kallgren, C. A., & Reno, R. R. (1991). A Focus Theory of Normative Conduct: A Theoretical Refinement and Reevaluation of the Role of Norms in Human Behavior. *Advances in Experimental Social Psychology, 24*(C), 201–234. https://doi.org/10.1016/S0065-2601(08)60330-5
Dawes, R. M. (1980). Social Dilemmas. *Annual Review of Psychology, 31*(1), 169–193. https://doi.org/10.1146/annurev.ps.31.020180.001125
Dawes, R. M. (1980). Social Dilemmas. *Annual Review of Psychology, 31*(1), 169–193. https://doi.org/10.1146/annurev.ps.31.020180.001125

Dawes, R. M. (1991). *Social Dilemmas, Economic Self-Interest, and Evolutionary Theory* (pp. 53–79). https://doi.org/10.1007/978-1-4612-3088-5_2

Dawes, R. M. (1991). *Social Dilemmas, Economic Self-Interest, and Evolutionary Theory* (pp. 53–79). https://doi.org/10.1007/978-1-4612-3088-5_2

Doron, I., Numhauser-Henning, A., Spanier, B., Georgantzi, N., & Mantovani, E. (2018). Ageism and Anti-Ageism in the Legal System: A Review of Key Themes. In *International Perspectives on Aging* (Vol. 19, pp. 303–319). Springer, Cham. https://doi.org/10.1007/978-3-319-73820-8_19

Doron, I., Numhauser-Henning, A., Spanier, B., Georgantzi, N., & Mantovani, E. (2018). Ageism and Anti-Ageism in the Legal System: A Review of Key Themes. In *International Perspectives on Aging* (Vol. 19, pp. 303–319). Springer, Cham. https://doi.org/10.1007/978-3-319-73820-8_19

Doron, I. I., Henning, A., Spainer, B., & Georgantzi, N. (n.d.). *(PDF) Ageism and Anti-Ageism in the Legal System: A Review of Key Themes*. Retrieved February 8, 2021, from https://www.researchgate.net/publication/3252890 46_Ageism_and_Anti-Ageism_in_the_Legal_System_A_Review_of_Ke y_Themes

Dufwenberg, M., & Kirchsteiger, G. (2004). A theory of sequential reciprocity. *Games and Economic Behavior, 47*(2), 268–298. https://doi.org/10.1016/j.geb.2003.06.003

Dufwenberg, M., & Kirchsteiger, G. (2004). A theory of sequential reciprocity. *Games and Economic*

Behavior, 47(2), 268–298.
https://doi.org/10.1016/j.geb.2003.06.003

ELÄKETURVAKESKUS. (n.d.). *Retirement Ages - Finnish Centre for Pensions*. Retrieved September 26, 2020, from https://www.etk.fi/en/work-and-pensions-abroad/international-comparisons/retirement-ages/

Ellingsen, T., Johannesson, M., Mollerstrom, J., & Munkhammar, S. (2012). Social framing effects: Preferences or beliefs? *Games and Economic Behavior, 76*(1), 117–130.
https://doi.org/10.1016/j.geb.2012.05.007

Ellingsen, T., Johannesson, M., Mollerstrom, J., & Munkhammar, S. (2012). Social framing effects: Preferences or beliefs? *Games and Economic Behavior, 76*(1), 117–130.
https://doi.org/10.1016/j.geb.2012.05.007

Elster, J. (1989). Social Norms and Economic Theory. *Journal of Economic Perspectives, 3*(4), 99–117.
https://doi.org/10.1257/jep.3.4.99

Elster, J. (1989). Social Norms and Economic Theory. *Journal of Economic Perspectives, 3*(4), 99–117.
https://doi.org/10.1257/jep.3.4.99

Elster, J. (1989). The Cement of Society. In *The Cement of Society*. Cambridge University Press.
https://doi.org/10.1017/cbo9780511624995

Elster, J. (1989). The Cement of Society. In *The Cement of Society*. Cambridge University Press.
https://doi.org/10.1017/cbo9780511624995

Falk, A., & Fischbacher, U. (2006). A theory of reciprocity. *Games and Economic Behavior, 54*(2), 293–315.
https://doi.org/10.1016/j.geb.2005.03.001

Falk, A., & Fischbacher, U. (2006). A theory of reciprocity. *Games and Economic Behavior, 54*(2), 293–315. https://doi.org/10.1016/j.geb.2005.03.001

Fallon, J. (2020). *Global Learner Survey.*

Fehr, E., & Schmidt, K. M. (1999). A theory of fairness, competition, and cooperation. *Quarterly Journal of Economics, 114*(3), 817–868. https://doi.org/10.1162/003355399556151

Fehr, E., & Schmidt, K. M. (1999). A theory of fairness, competition, and cooperation. *Quarterly Journal of Economics, 114*(3), 817–868. https://doi.org/10.1162/003355399556151

Fehr, E., & Schmidt, K. M. (2006). Chapter 8 The Economics of Fairness, Reciprocity and Altruism - Experimental Evidence and New Theories. In *Handbook of the Economics of Giving, Altruism and Reciprocity* (Vol. 1, pp. 615–691). https://doi.org/10.1016/S1574-0714(06)01008-6

Fehr, E., & Schmidt, K. M. (2006). Chapter 8 The Economics of Fairness, Reciprocity and Altruism - Experimental Evidence and New Theories. In *Handbook of the Economics of Giving, Altruism and Reciprocity* (Vol. 1, pp. 615–691). https://doi.org/10.1016/S1574-0714(06)01008-6

Finnish Centre for Pensions ELÄKETURVAKESKUS. (n.d.). *Retirement Ages - Finnish Centre for Pensions*. Retrieved September 26, 2020, from https://www.etk.fi/en/work-and-pensions-abroad/international-comparisons/retirement-ages/

Fletcher, A. (2016). *Understanding the Causes of Age Discrimination – Freechild Institute*. Freechild

Institute. https://freechild.org/2016/01/07/age-discrimination/

Fletcher, A. (2016). *Understanding the Causes of Age Discrimination – Freechild Institute*. Freechild Institute . https://freechild.org/2016/01/07/age-discrimination/

Freeman, L. C., & Ataöv, T. (1960). Invalidity of indirect and direct measures of attitude toward cheating. *Journal of Personality, 28*(4), 443–447. https://doi.org/10.1111/j.1467-6494.1960.tb01631.x

Freeman, L. C., & Ataöv, T. (1960). Invalidity of indirect and direct measures of attitude toward cheating. *Journal of Personality, 28*(4), 443–447. https://doi.org/10.1111/j.1467-6494.1960.tb01631.x

Gächter, S., Nosenzo, D., & Sefton, M. (2013). Peer effects in pro-social behavior: Social norms or social preferences? *Journal of the European Economic Association, 11*(3), 548–573. https://doi.org/10.1111/jeea.12015

Gächter, S., Nosenzo, D., & Sefton, M. (2013). Peer effects in pro-social behavior: Social norms or social preferences? *Journal of the European Economic Association, 11*(3), 548–573. https://doi.org/10.1111/jeea.12015

Geanakoplos, J., Pearce, D., & Stacchetti, E. (1989). Psychological games and sequential rationality. *Games and Economic Behavior, 1*(1), 60–79. https://doi.org/10.1016/0899-8256(89)90005-5

Geanakoplos, J., Pearce, D., & Stacchetti, E. (1989). Psychological games and sequential rationality.

Games and Economic Behavior, *1*(1), 60–79.
https://doi.org/10.1016/0899-8256(89)90005-5

Government of India. (2020). *National Education Policy 2020 Ministry of Human Resource Development Government of India.*

Granovetter, M. (1985). Economic Action and Social Structure: The Problem of Embeddedness. *American Journal of Sociology*, *91*(3), 481–510. https://doi.org/10.1086/228311

Granovetter, M. (1985). Economic Action and Social Structure: The Problem of Embeddedness. *American Journal of Sociology*, *91*(3), 481–510. https://doi.org/10.1086/228311

Gurchiek, K. (n.d.). *Is Age a Part of Your Inclusion Strategy?* Retrieved February 8, 2021, from https://www.shrm.org/resourcesandtools/hr-topics/global-hr/pages/welcoming-older-workers.aspx?_ga=2.62544421.809543629.156615 5604-920689375.1491920969

Hamilton, W. D. (1964). The genetical evolution of social behaviour. I. *Journal of Theoretical Biology*, *7*(1), 1–16. https://doi.org/10.1016/0022-5193(64)90038-4

Hamilton, W. D. (1964). The genetical evolution of social behaviour. I. *Journal of Theoretical Biology*, *7*(1), 1–16. https://doi.org/10.1016/0022-5193(64)90038-4

Hamilton, W. D. (1964). The genetical evolution of social behaviour. II. *Journal of Theoretical Biology*, *7*(1), 17–52. https://doi.org/10.1016/0022-5193(64)90039-6

Hamilton, W. D. (1964). The genetical evolution of social behaviour. II. *Journal of Theoretical*

Biology, 7(1), 17–52. https://doi.org/10.1016/0022-5193(64)90039-6

Hausman, D. M. (2008). Fairness and social norms. *Philosophy of Science, 75*(5), 850–860. https://doi.org/10.1086/594529

Hausman, D. M. (2008). Fairness and social norms. *Philosophy of Science, 75*(5), 850–860. https://doi.org/10.1086/594529

Henrich, J., & Boyd, R. (2001). Why people punish defectors: Weak conformist transmission can stabilize costly enforcement of norms in cooperative dilemmas. *Journal of Theoretical Biology, 208*(1), 79–89. https://doi.org/10.1006/jtbi.2000.2202

Henrich, J., & Boyd, R. (2001). Why people punish defectors: Weak conformist transmission can stabilize costly enforcement of norms in cooperative dilemmas. *Journal of Theoretical Biology, 208*(1), 79–89. https://doi.org/10.1006/jtbi.2000.2202

Henrich, J., Boyd, R., Bowles, S., Camerer, C., Fehr, E., Gintis, H., & McElreath, R. (2001). In search of Homo economicus: Behavioral experiments in 15 small-scale societies. *American Economic Review, 91*(2), 73–84. https://doi.org/10.1257/aer.91.2.73

Henrich, J., Boyd, R., Bowles, S., Camerer, C., Fehr, E., Gintis, H., & McElreath, R. (2001). In search of Homo economicus: Behavioral experiments in 15 small-scale societies. *American Economic Review, 91*(2), 73–84. https://doi.org/10.1257/aer.91.2.73

Holon IQ. (2020). *Global Education Conditions Survey | HolonIQ*. HolonIQ - Global Education Outlook Survey. https://globaloutlook.holoniq.com/

Insko, C. A., & Schopler, J. (1967). Triadic Consistency: A statement of affective-cognitive-conative consistency. *Psychological Review, 74*(5), 361–376. https://doi.org/10.1037/h0020278

Insko, C. A., & Schopler, J. (1967). Triadic Consistency: A statement of affective-cognitive-conative consistency. *Psychological Review, 74*(5), 361–376. https://doi.org/10.1037/h0020278

Kapoor, K. (2019). *Is Age an Issue in Indian Workplaces in India?* https://www.entrepreneur.com/article/333315

Kapoor, K. (2019). *Is Age an Issue in Indian Workplaces in India?* https://www.entrepreneur.com/article/333315

Kramer, R. M., & Brewer, M. B. (1984). Effects of group identity on resource use in a simulated commons dilemma. *Journal of Personality and Social Psychology, 46*(5), 1044–1057. https://doi.org/10.1037/0022-3514.46.5.1044

Kramer, R. M., & Brewer, M. B. (1984). Effects of group identity on resource use in a simulated commons dilemma. *Journal of Personality and Social Psychology, 46*(5), 1044–1057. https://doi.org/10.1037/0022-3514.46.5.1044

Krupka, E. L., & Weber, R. A. (2013). Identifying social norms using coordination games: Why does dictator game sharing vary? *Journal of the European Economic Association, 11*(3), 495–524. https://doi.org/10.1111/jeea.12006

Krupka, E. L., & Weber, R. A. (2013). Identifying social norms using coordination games: Why does dictator game sharing vary? *Journal of the*

European Economic Association, 11(3), 495–524.
https://doi.org/10.1111/jeea.12006

Lapiere, R. T. (1934). Attitudes vs. Actions. *Social Forces, 13*(2), 230–237.
https://doi.org/10.2307/2570339

Lapiere, R. T. (1934). Attitudes vs. Actions. *Social Forces, 13*(2), 230–237.
https://doi.org/10.2307/2570339

Lev, S., Wurm, S., & Ayalon, L. (2018). Origins of Ageism at the Individual Level. In *International Perspectives on Aging* (Vol. 19, pp. 51–72). Springer, Cham. https://doi.org/10.1007/978-3-319-73820-8_4

Lewis, D. (2008). Convention: A Philosophical Study. In *Convention: A Philosophical Study*. Wiley Blackwell. https://doi.org/10.1002/9780470693711

Lewis, D. (2008). Convention: A Philosophical Study. In *Convention: A Philosophical Study*. Wiley Blackwell. https://doi.org/10.1002/9780470693711

Li, C., & Lalani, F. (2020). *The rise of online learning during the COVID-19 pandemic | World Economic Forum*. World Economic Forum. https://www.weforum.org/agenda/2020/04/coronavirus-education-global-covid19-online-digital-learning/

López-Pérez, R. (2008). Aversion to norm-breaking: A model. *Games and Economic Behavior, 64*(1), 237–267.
https://doi.org/10.1016/j.geb.2007.10.009

López-Pérez, R. (2008). Aversion to norm-breaking: A model. *Games and Economic Behavior, 64*(1), 237–267.
https://doi.org/10.1016/j.geb.2007.10.009

Lydia, D. (n.d.). *Ageism is thriving, so what are companies doing about it?* Retrieved February 8, 2021, from https://www.fastcompany.com/90325055/ageism-is-thriving-so-what-are-companies-doing-about-it

Mackie, G. (1996). Ending footbinding and infibulation: A convention account. *American Sociological Review, 61*(6), 999–1017. https://doi.org/10.2307/2096305

Mackie, G. (1996). Ending footbinding and infibulation: A convention account. *American Sociological Review, 61*(6), 999–1017. https://doi.org/10.2307/2096305

Maddox, G. (2001). The Encyclopedia of Aging. In *The Encyclopedia of Aging*. Springer Berlin Heidelberg. https://doi.org/10.1007/978-3-662-38338-4

Marcus, B. (n.d.). *The next #MeToo movement: Older women confront ageism - Chicago Tribune.* Retrieved February 8, 2021, from https://www.chicagotribune.com/opinion/commentary/ct-perspec-metoo-ageism-older-women-discrimination-0321-20190320-story.html

Miller, D. T., & Ratner, R. K. (1996). *The Power of the Myth of Self-Interest* (pp. 25–48). https://doi.org/10.1007/978-1-4757-9927-9_3

Miller, D. T., & Ratner, R. K. (1996). *The Power of the Myth of Self-Interest* (pp. 25–48). https://doi.org/10.1007/978-1-4757-9927-9_3

Mortimer, C. (2015). *World minimum marriage age: Chart shows the lowest age you can legally get married around the world | The Independent | The Independent.*

https://www.independent.co.uk/news/world/lowest
-age-you-can-legally-get-married-around-world-
10415517.html

Mortimer, C. (n.d.). *World minimum marriage age:
Chart shows the lowest age you can legally get
married around the world | The Independent | The
Independent*. The Independent. Retrieved February
8, 2021, from
https://www.independent.co.uk/news/world/lowest
-age-you-can-legally-get-married-around-world-
10415517.html

Nachbar, J. H. (1990). "Evolutionary" selection
dynamics in games: Convergence and limit
properties. *International Journal of Game Theory*,
19(1), 59–89. https://doi.org/10.1007/BF01753708

Nachbar, J. H. (1990). "Evolutionary" selection
dynamics in games: Convergence and limit
properties. *International Journal of Game Theory*,
19(1), 59–89. https://doi.org/10.1007/BF01753708

North, D. C. (1990). A Transaction Cost Theory of
Politics. *Journal of Theoretical Politics*, *2*(4), 355–
367.
https://doi.org/10.1177/0951692890002004001

North, D. C. (1990). A Transaction Cost Theory of
Politics. *Journal of Theoretical Politics*, *2*(4), 355–
367.
https://doi.org/10.1177/0951692890002004001

O'gorman, H. J. (1975). Pluralistic ignorance and white
estimates of white support for racial segregation.
Public Opinion Quarterly, *39*(3), 313–330.
https://doi.org/10.1086/268231

O'gorman, H. J. (1975). Pluralistic ignorance and white
estimates of white support for racial segregation.

Public Opinion Quarterly, *39*(3), 313–330.
https://doi.org/10.1086/268231

Ostrom, E. (2000). Collective action and the evolution of social norms. *Journal of Economic Perspectives*, *14*(3), 137–158. https://doi.org/10.1257/jep.14.3.137

Ostrom, E. (2000). Collective action and the evolution of social norms. *Journal of Economic Perspectives*, *14*(3), 137–158. https://doi.org/10.1257/jep.14.3.137

Palmore, E. (2001). The Ageism Survey: First findings. In *Gerontologist* (Vol. 41, Issue 5, pp. 572–575). Gerontological Society of America. https://doi.org/10.1093/geront/41.5.572

Palmore, E. B. (1999). *Ageism: Negative and Positive, 2nd Edition - Erdman Palmore, PhD - Google Books*. https://books.google.co.in/books?hl=en&lr=&id=7ZbSCgAAQBAJ&oi=fnd&pg=PR5&dq=positive+ageism+definition+&ots=o0yEs4Tnis&sig=wAq1L5ven_gkM1Yqsdj064DYLwU#v=onepage&q=positive ageism definition&f=false

Palmore, E. (1999). *Ageism: Negative and Positive, 2nd Edition - Erdman Palmore, PhD - Google Books*. https://books.google.co.in/books/about/Ageism.html?id=Cg4_DTUuV4IC&redir_esc=y

Palmore, E. (2001). The Ageism Survey. *The Gerontologist*, *41*(5), 572–575. https://doi.org/10.1093/geront/41.5.572

Prentice, D. A., & Miller, D. T. (1993). Pluralistic Ignorance and Alcohol Use on Campus: Some Consequences of Misperceiving the Social Norm. *Journal of Personality and Social Psychology*,

64(2), 243–256. https://doi.org/10.1037/0022-3514.64.2.243

Prentice, D. A., & Miller, D. T. (1993). Pluralistic Ignorance and Alcohol Use on Campus: Some Consequences of Misperceiving the Social Norm. *Journal of Personality and Social Psychology*, *64*(2), 243–256. https://doi.org/10.1037/0022-3514.64.2.243

Protière, C., Viens, P., Rousseau, F., & Moatti, J. P. (2010). Prescribers' attitudes toward elderly breast cancer patients. Discrimination or empathy? In *Critical Reviews in Oncology/Hematology* (Vol. 75, Issue 2, pp. 138–150). Crit Rev Oncol Hematol. https://doi.org/10.1016/j.critrevonc.2009.09.007

Reuben, E., & Riedl, A. (2013). Enforcement of contribution norms in public good games with heterogeneous populations. *Games and Economic Behavior*, *77*(1), 122–137. https://doi.org/10.1016/j.geb.2012.10.001

Reuben, E., & Riedl, A. (2013). Enforcement of contribution norms in public good games with heterogeneous populations. *Games and Economic Behavior*, *77*(1), 122–137. https://doi.org/10.1016/j.geb.2012.10.001

S M Fazalali. (n.d.). *Air India Etc. Etc vs Nergesh Meerza & Ors. Etc. Etc on 28 August, 1981*. Retrieved October 4, 2020, from https://indiankanoon.org/doc/1903603/

Sage Publications. (n.d.). *Aging and Ageism: Cultural Influences Learning Objectives*.

SAGE Publications, I. (2018). *Aging and Ageism: Cultural Influences Learning Objectives*.

Schram, A., & Charness, G. (2015). Inducing social norms in laboratory allocation choices. *Management Science, 61*(7), 1531–1546. https://doi.org/10.1287/mnsc.2014.2073

Schram, A., & Charness, G. (2015). Inducing social norms in laboratory allocation choices. *Management Science, 61*(7), 1531–1546. https://doi.org/10.1287/mnsc.2014.2073

Schroyen, S., Adam, S., Jerusalem, G., & Missotten, P. (2014). Ageism and its clinical impact in oncogeriatry: State of knowledge and therapeutic leads. *Clinical Interventions in Aging, 10*, 117–125. https://doi.org/10.2147/CIA.S70942

Skyrms, B. (1996). Evolution of the Social Contract. In *Evolution of the Social Contract*. Cambridge University Press. https://doi.org/10.1017/cbo9780511806308

Skyrms, B. (1996). Evolution of the Social Contract. In *Evolution of the Social Contract*. Cambridge University Press. https://doi.org/10.1017/cbo9780511806308

Skyrms, B. (2003). The stag hunt and the evolution of social structure. In *The Stag Hunt and the Evolution of Social Structure*. Cambridge University Press. https://doi.org/10.1017/CBO9781139165228

Skyrms, B. (2003). The stag hunt and the evolution of social structure. In *The Stag Hunt and the Evolution of Social Structure*. Cambridge University Press. https://doi.org/10.1017/CBO9781139165228

Smith, A. (2019). *Workers Around the Globe Face Age Discrimination.*

https://www.shrm.org/resourcesandtools/legal-and-compliance/employment-law/pages/global-age-discrimination.aspx

Smith, J. M., & Price, G. R. (1973). The logic of animal conflict. *Nature, 246*(5427), 15–18. https://doi.org/10.1038/246015a0

Smith, J. M., & Price, G. R. (1973). The logic of animal conflict. *Nature, 246*(5427), 15–18. https://doi.org/10.1038/246015a0

Stypinska, J., & Turek, K. (2017). Hard and soft age discrimination: the dual nature of workplace discrimination. *European Journal of Ageing, 14*(1), 49–61. https://doi.org/10.1007/s10433-016-0407-y

Stypinska, J., & Turek, K. (2017). Hard and soft age discrimination: the dual nature of workplace discrimination. *European Journal of Ageing, 14*(1), 49–61. https://doi.org/10.1007/s10433-016-0407-y

Sugden, R. (2000). The Motivating Power of Expectations. In *Rationality, Rules, and Structure* (pp. 103–129). Springer Netherlands. https://doi.org/10.1007/978-94-015-9616-9_7

Sugden, R. (2000). The Motivating Power of Expectations. In *Rationality, Rules, and Structure* (pp. 103–129). Springer Netherlands. https://doi.org/10.1007/978-94-015-9616-9_7

Swift, H. J., Abrams, D., & Lamont, R. A. (2019). Ageism Around the World. In *Encyclopedia of Gerontology and Population Aging* (pp. 1–12). Springer International Publishing. https://doi.org/10.1007/978-3-319-69892-2_586-1

Swift, H. J., Abrams, D., & Lamont, R. A. (2019). Ageism Around the World. In *Encyclopedia of Gerontology and Population Aging* (pp. 1–12). Springer International Publishing. https://doi.org/10.1007/978-3-319-69892-2_586-1

Swift, H. J., Abrams, D., & Lamont, R. A. (2019). Ageism Around the World. In *Encyclopedia of Gerontology and Population Aging* (pp. 1–12). Springer International Publishing. https://doi.org/10.1007/978-3-319-69892-2_586-1

Swift, H. J., Abrams, D., & Lamont, R. A. (2019). Ageism Around the World. In *Encyclopedia of Gerontology and Population Aging* (pp. 1–12). Springer International Publishing. https://doi.org/10.1007/978-3-319-69892-2_586-1

Taylor, P. D., & Jonker, L. B. (1978). Evolutionary stable strategies and game dynamics. *Mathematical Biosciences*, *40*(1–2), 145–156. https://doi.org/10.1016/0025-5564(78)90077-9

Taylor, P. D., & Jonker, L. B. (1978). Evolutionary stable strategies and game dynamics. *Mathematical Biosciences*, *40*(1–2), 145–156. https://doi.org/10.1016/0025-5564(78)90077-9

Trivers, R. L. (1971). The Evolution of Reciprocal Altruism. *The Quarterly Review of Biology*, *46*(1), 35–57. https://doi.org/10.1086/406755

Trivers, R. L. (1971). The Evolution of Reciprocal Altruism. *The Quarterly Review of Biology*, *46*(1), 35–57. https://doi.org/10.1086/406755

Tumanishvili, G. G. (2016). Law - a Natural Phenomenon or a Manmade System? in the Light of New Understanding of the Origin of Law. *Education Sciences and Psychology*, *4*, 122–141.

U.S. Department of Labor. (n.d.). *Age Discrimination | U.S. Department of Labor*. Retrieved October 4, 2020, from https://www.dol.gov/general/topic/discrimination/agedisc

U.S. Equal Employment Opportunity Commission. (n.d.). *Age Discrimination | U.S. Equal Employment Opportunity Commission*. Retrieved October 4, 2020, from https://www.eeoc.gov/age-discrimination

United Nations. (1982). *STATISTICAL PAPERS Series M No.74*.

Vanderschraaf, P. (1995). Convention as correlated equilibrium. *Erkenntnis, 42*(1), 65–87. https://doi.org/10.1007/BF01666812

Vanderschraaf, P. (1995). Convention as correlated equilibrium. *Erkenntnis, 42*(1), 65–87. https://doi.org/10.1007/BF01666812

Warner, L. G., & DeFleur, M. L. (1969). Attitude as an interactional concept: social constraint and social distance as intervening variables between attitudes and action. *American Sociological Review, 34*(2), 153–169. https://doi.org/10.2307/2092174

Warner, L. G., & DeFleur, M. L. (1969). Attitude as an interactional concept: social constraint and social distance as intervening variables between attitudes and action. *American Sociological Review, 34*(2), 153–169. https://doi.org/10.2307/2092174

WHO. (2015). *Ageing and Health unit*. WHO . https://www.who.int/teams/maternal-newborn-child-adolescent-health-and-ageing/ageing-and-health

Wicker, A. W. (1969). Attitudes versus Actions: The Relationship of Verbal and Overt Behavioral Responses to Attitude Objects. *Journal of Social Issues*, *25*(4), 41–78. https://doi.org/10.1111/j.1540-4560.1969.tb00619.x

Wicker, A. W. (1969). Attitudes versus Actions: The Relationship of Verbal and Overt Behavioral Responses to Attitude Objects. *Journal of Social Issues*, *25*(4), 41–78. https://doi.org/10.1111/j.1540-4560.1969.tb00619.x

Winton, R. (2019). *Jury awards former Times sports columnist $15.4 million - Los Angeles Times*. Los Angeles Times. https://www.latimes.com/california/story/2019-08-19/jury-awards-tj-simers-former-times-sports-columnist-15-4-million

Winton, R. (2019). *Jury awards former Times sports columnist $15.4 million - Los Angeles Times*. https://www.latimes.com/california/story/2019-08-19/jury-awards-tj-simers-former-times-sports-columnist-15-4-million

Witt, J. (n.d.). *The Law of Salus Populi | The Yale Review*. Retrieved February 8, 2021, from https://yalereview.yale.edu/law-salus-populi

Witt, J. (n.d.). *The Law of Salus Populi | The Yale Review*. Retrieved February 8, 2021, from https://yalereview.yale.edu/law-salus-populi

Wrong, D. H. (1961). The Oversocialized Conception of Man in Modern Sociology. *American Sociological Review*, *26*(2), 183. https://doi.org/10.2307/2089854

Wrong, D. H. (1961). The Oversocialized Conception of Man in Modern Sociology. *American Sociological Review, 26*(2), 183. https://doi.org/10.2307/2089854

Xiao, E., & Bicchieri, C. (2010). When equality trumps reciprocity. *Journal of Economic Psychology, 31*(3), 456–470. https://doi.org/10.1016/j.joep.2010.02.001

Xiao, E., & Bicchieri, C. (2010). When equality trumps reciprocity. *Journal of Economic Psychology, 31*(3), 456–470. https://doi.org/10.1016/j.joep.2010.02.001

Young, E. (n.d.). *Most Older Americans Face Age Discrimination in the Workplace, New Survey Finds – Working Longer*. Retrieved February 8, 2021, from https://workinglongerstudy.org/most-older-americans-face-age-discrimination-in-the-workplace%2C-new-survey-finds/

Young, H. P. (1998). Social norms and economic welfare. *European Economic Review, 42*(3–5), 821–830. https://doi.org/10.1016/s0014-2921(97)00138-4

Young, H. P. (1998). Social norms and economic welfare. *European Economic Review, 42*(3–5), 821–830. https://doi.org/10.1016/s0014-2921(97)00138-4

Young, H. P. (1993). The Evolution of Conventions. *Econometrica, 61*(1), 57. https://doi.org/10.2307/2951778

Young, H. P. (1993). The Evolution of Conventions. *Econometrica, 61*(1), 57. https://doi.org/10.2307/2951778

World minimum marriage age: Chart shows the lowest age you can legally get married around the world | The Independent | The Independent. (n.d.). Retrieved February 8, 2021, from https://www.independent.co.uk/news/world/lowest -age-you-can-legally-get-married-around-world-10415517.html

Working Better with Age: Switzerland-Assessment and recommendations © OECD Directorate for Employment, Labour and Social Affairs Employment Working Better with Age SWITZERLAND Assessment and main recommandations. (2014).

Working Better with Age: Switzerland-Assessment and recommendations © OECD Directorate for Employment, Labour and Social Affairs Employment Working Better with Age SWITZERLAND Assessment and main recommandations. (2014).

Working Better with Age: Switzerland-Assessment and recommendations © OECD Directorate for Employment, Labour and Social Affairs Employment Working Better with Age SWITZERLAND Assessment and main recommandations. (2014).

Why choose educations.com for your student recruitment needs? (n.d.). International Student Recruitment . Retrieved January 8, 2021, from https://institutions.educations.com/

WESTERN AIR LINES, INC., Petitioner, v. Charles G. CRISWELL et al. | Supreme Court | US Law | LII / Legal Information Institute. (n.d.). Retrieved February 8, 2021, from

https://www.law.cornell.edu/supremecourt/text/47
2/400

*Understanding the Causes of Age Discrimination –
Freechild Institute.* (n.d.). Retrieved February 8,
2021, from https://freechild.org/2016/01/07/age-
discrimination/

*Understanding the Causes of Age Discrimination –
Freechild Institute.* (n.d.). Retrieved February 8,
2021, from https://freechild.org/2016/01/07/age-
discrimination/

*Understanding the Causes of Age Discrimination –
Freechild Institute.* (n.d.). Retrieved February 8,
2021, from https://freechild.org/2016/01/07/age-
discrimination/

Ubi jus ibi remedium - Oxford Reference. (n.d.).
Retrieved February 8, 2021, from
https://www.oxfordreference.com/view/10.1093/oi
/authority.20110803110448446

Ubi jus ibi remedium - Oxford Reference. (2021).
Oxford University Press .
https://www.oxfordreference.com/view/10.1093/oi
/authority.20110803110448446

Ubi jus ibi remedium - Oxford Reference. (n.d.).
Retrieved February 8, 2021, from
https://www.oxfordreference.com/view/10.1093/oi
/authority.20110803110448446

Ubi jus ibi remedium - Oxford Reference. (n.d.). Oxford
Reference . Retrieved February 8, 2021, from
https://www.oxfordreference.com/view/10.1093/oi
/authority.20110803110448446

*TRANS WORLD AIRLINES, INC., Petitioner, v. Harold
H. THURSTON et al. AIR LINE PILOTS
ASSOCIATION, INTERNATIONAL, Petitioner, v.*

Harold H. THURSTON et al. | Supreme Court | US Law | LII / Legal Information Institute. (n.d.). Retrieved February 8, 2021, from https://www.law.cornell.edu/supremecourt/text/469/111

The Law of Salus Populi | The Yale Review. (n.d.). The Yale Review . Retrieved February 8, 2021, from https://yalereview.yale.edu/law-salus-populi

The Encyclopedia of Aging. (2001). In *The Encyclopedia of Aging*. Springer Berlin Heidelberg. https://doi.org/10.1007/978-3-662-38338-4

Social Norms (Stanford Encyclopedia of Philosophy/Winter 2018 Edition). (n.d.). Retrieved February 8, 2021, from https://plato.stanford.edu/archives/win2018/entries/social-norms/

Social Norms (Stanford Encyclopedia of Philosophy/Winter 2018 Edition). (2011). Stanford Encyclopedia of Philosophy. https://plato.stanford.edu/archives/win2018/entries/social-norms/

Social Image and the 50-50 Norm: A Theoretical and Experimental Analysis of Audience Effects. (2009). *Econometrica, 77*(5), 1607–1636. https://doi.org/10.3982/ecta7384

Russian Federation. LABOR CODE OF THE RUSSIAN FEDERATION OF 31 DECEMBER 2001. (n.d.). Retrieved February 8, 2021, from http://www.ilo.org/dyn/natlex/docs/WEBTEXT/60535/65252/E01RUS01.ht#chap62

Russian Federation. LABOR CODE OF THE RUSSIAN FEDERATION OF 31 DECEMBER 2001. (n.d.).

Retrieved February 8, 2021, from
http://www.ilo.org/dyn/natlex/docs/WEBTEXT/60
535/65252/E01RUS01.ht#chap62

*Russian Federation. LABOR CODE OF THE RUSSIAN
FEDERATION OF 31 DECEMBER 2001.* (n.d.).
Retrieved February 8, 2021, from
http://www.ilo.org/dyn/natlex/docs/WEBTEXT/60
535/65252/E01RUS01.ht#chap62

Russia — age discrimination. (n.d.). Retrieved February
8, 2021, from
http://www.agediscrimination.info/international-
age-discrimination/russia

Russia — age discrimination. (n.d.). Retrieved February
8, 2021, from
http://www.agediscrimination.info/international-
age-discrimination/russia

Retirement Ages - Finnish Centre for Pensions. (n.d.).
Retrieved February 8, 2021, from
https://www.etk.fi/en/work-and-pensions-
abroad/international-comparisons/retirement-ages/

Retirement Ages - Finnish Centre for Pensions. (n.d.).
Finnish Centre for Pensions. Retrieved February 8,
2021, from https://www.etk.fi/en/work-and-
pensions-abroad/international-
comparisons/retirement-ages/

*Provisional Guidelines on Standard International Age
Classifications.* (n.d.). Retrieved February 8, 2021,
from
https://unstats.un.org/unsd/publication/SeriesM/Ser
iesM_74e.pdf

*Presidents, Vice Presidents, and First Ladies of the
United States | USAGov.* (n.d.). USAGov.

Retrieved February 8, 2021, from
https://www.usa.gov/presidents

*Jury awards former Times sports columnist $15.4
million - Los Angeles Times*. (n.d.). Retrieved
February 8, 2021, from
https://www.latimes.com/california/story/2019-08-
19/jury-awards-tj-simers-former-times-sports-
columnist-15-4-million

Is Age an Issue in Indian Workplaces in India? (n.d.).
Retrieved February 8, 2021, from
https://www.entrepreneur.com/article/333315

Is Age a Part of Your Inclusion Strategy? (n.d.).
Retrieved February 8, 2021, from
https://www.shrm.org/resourcesandtools/hr-
topics/global-hr/pages/welcoming-older-
workers.aspx?_ga=2.62544421.809543629.156615
5604-920689375.1491920969

Is Age a Part of Your Inclusion Strategy? (n.d.).
Retrieved February 8, 2021, from
https://www.shrm.org/resourcesandtools/hr-
topics/global-hr/pages/welcoming-older-
workers.aspx?_ga=2.62544421.809543629.156615
5604-920689375.1491920969

*Indian Council Of Legal Aid & Advice Vs. Bar Council
Of India on 17 January, 1995 - Legitquest*. (n.d.).
Retrieved February 8, 2021, from
https://www.legitquest.com/case/indian-council-
of-legal-aid-advice-v-bar-council-of-india/ee2

*Indian Council Of Legal Aid & Advice Vs. Bar Council
Of India on 17 January, 1995 - Legitquest*. (n.d.).
Retrieved February 8, 2021, from
https://www.legitquest.com/case/indian-council-
of-legal-aid-advice-v-bar-council-of-india/ee2

Indian Council Of Legal Aid & Advice Vs. Bar Council Of India on 17 January, 1995 - Legitquest. (n.d.). Retrieved February 8, 2021, from https://www.legitquest.com/case/indian-council-of-legal-aid-advice-v-bar-council-of-india/ee2

Google Chrome.app. (n.d.).

Election - Election Commission of India. (n.d.). Election Commission of India. Retrieved February 8, 2021, from https://eci.gov.in/elections/election/

Deja Vu: Google Settles Age Discrimination Lawsuit For $11 Million. (n.d.). Retrieved February 8, 2021, from https://www.forbes.com/sites/patriciagbarnes/2019/07/20/deja-vu-google-settles-age-discrimination-lawsuit-for-11-million/?sh=70aeb34971f1

Constitution of India. (n.d.). Retrieved February 8, 2021, from https://www.constitutionofindia.net/constitution_of_india/fundamental_rights/articles/Article 15

Constitution of India. (n.d.). Retrieved October 4, 2020, from https://www.constitutionofindia.net/constitution_of_india/fundamental_rights/articles/Article 15

Constitution of India. (n.d.). Constitution of India . Retrieved October 4, 2020, from https://www.constitutionofindia.net/constitution_of_india/fundamental_rights/articles

Constitution of India. (n.d.). Retrieved February 8, 2021, from https://www.constitutionofindia.net/constitution_of_india/fundamental_rights/articles/Article 15

CHILD MARRIAGE AND THE LAW - Girls Not Brides. (n.d.). Girls Not Brides . Retrieved February 8,

2021, from https://www.girlsnotbrides.org/child-marriage-law/

Air India Etc. Etc vs Nergesh Meerza & Ors. Etc. Etc on 28 August, 1981. (n.d.). Retrieved February 8, 2021, from https://indiankanoon.org/doc/1903603/?__cf_chl_j schl_tk__=58dcbb27af647c2dc9fe11d331c96bc9fa f52b07-1612796435-0-AWXEiCUaZ9GhhdISVIyqShGBN7x3ZITb08Iq XpGXDYHotIt2OAXBX83pA6fJDqKbtvVCmOX X8NXciFyXzx0n8rJR3MvwTMh_UQIFEpWCl4 R44hoQwLWKeiHJG6j0HKR4LFHalfQcDMyzsE nUrtOpARZikYXoxSMRKLZWEB9mkLFN5AD gzPhSOMR1HJpUNYGjhI-V4BiQA2CL_yBYlMiIMYm7pm692XiPioV7nZ mfBRG6cunK6PT_QLGmKNGBj8KX__m7uzbE Sh1SYff9_UMC0rue_4Kt3pdgGNLsZFNNYiKU QEa13Lkr9IKUH33YYN66iFsVgtLqV-yDrkdBo0ENAnESYzoyJJ5z3w87Rn4ctZZRCLz-8_-lOemk8xjMGRWAjQ

Air India Etc. Etc vs Nergesh Meerza & Ors. Etc. Etc on 28 August, 1981. (n.d.). Retrieved February 8, 2021, from https://indiankanoon.org/doc/1903603/

Air India Etc. Etc vs Nergesh Meerza & Ors. Etc. Etc on 28 August, 1981. (n.d.). Retrieved February 8, 2021, from https://indiankanoon.org/doc/1903603/?__cf_chl_j schl_tk__=58dcbb27af647c2dc9fe11d331c96bc9fa f52b07-1612796435-0-AWXEiCUaZ9GhhdISVIyqShGBN7x3ZITb08Iq XpGXDYHotIt2OAXBX83pA6fJDqKbtvVCmOX X8NXciFyXzx0n8rJR3MvwTMh_UQIFEpWCl4 R44hoQwLWKeiHJG6j0HKR4LFHalfQcDMyzsE

nUrtOpARZikYXoxSMRKLZWEB9mkLFN5AD
gzPhSOMR1HJpUNYGjhI-
V4BiQA2CL_yBYlMiIMYm7pm692XiPioV7nZ
mfBRG6cunK6PT_QLGmKNGBj8KX__m7uzbE
Sh1SYff9_UMC0rue_4Kt3pdgGNLsZFNNYiKU
QEa13Lkr9IKUH33YYN66iFsVgtLqV-
yDrkdBo0ENAnESYzoyJJ5z3w87Rn4ctZZRCLz-
8_-lOemk8xjMGRWAjQ

*Aging and Ageism: Cultural Influences Learning
Objectives.* (n.d.). Retrieved February 8, 2021,
from
https://us.sagepub.com/sites/default/files/upm-
assets/90251_book_item_90251.pdf

*Age Discrimination | U.S. Equal Employment
Opportunity Commission.* (n.d.). Retrieved
February 8, 2021, from https://www.eeoc.gov/age-
discrimination

*Age Discrimination | U.S. Equal Employment
Opportunity Commission.* (n.d.). Retrieved
February 8, 2021, from https://www.eeoc.gov/age-
discrimination

*Age Discrimination | U.S. Equal Employment
Opportunity Commission.* (n.d.). U.S. Equal
Employment Opportunity Commission. Retrieved
February 8, 2021, from https://www.eeoc.gov/age-
discrimination

Age Discrimination | U.S. Department of Labor. (n.d.).
Retrieved February 8, 2021, from
https://www.dol.gov/general/topic/discrimination/a
gedisc

Age Discrimination | U.S. Department of Labor. (n.d.).
Retrieved February 8, 2021, from

https://www.dol.gov/general/topic/discrimination/a
gedisc

Age Discrimination - Landmark Discrimination Cases - Pilots, Adea, Flight, and Court - JRank Articles. (n.d.). Retrieved February 8, 2021, from https://law.jrank.org/pages/4166/Age-Discrimination-Landmark-Discrimination-Cases.html

Age Discrimination - Landmark Discrimination Cases - Pilots, Adea, Flight, and Court - JRank Articles. (n.d.). Retrieved February 8, 2021, from https://law.jrank.org/pages/4166/Age-Discrimination-Landmark-Discrimination-Cases.html

Age Discrimination - Landmark Discrimination Cases - Pilots, Adea, Flight, and Court - JRank Articles. (n.d.). Web Solutions LLC . Retrieved February 8, 2021, from https://law.jrank.org/pages/4166/Age-Discrimination-Landmark-Discrimination-Cases.html

www.ingramcontent.com/pod-product-compliance
Lightning Source LLC
Chambersburg PA
CBHW071757150726
47998CB00005B/1979